90 DAYS TO SUCCESS IN CONSULTING

William McKnight

Course Technology PTR
A part of Cengage Learning

COURSE TECHNOLOGY
CENGAGE Learning™

Australia, Brazil, Japan, Korea, Mexico, Singapore, Spain, United Kingdom, United States

COURSE TECHNOLOGY
CENGAGE Learning™

90 Days to Success in Consulting
William McKnight

Publisher and General Manager, Course Technology PTR:
Stacy L. Hiquet

Associate Director of Marketing:
Sarah Panella

Manager of Editorial Services:
Heather Talbot

Marketing Manager:
Mark Hughes

Acquisitions Editor:
Mitzi Koontz

Project Editor/Copy Editor:
Cathleen D. Small

Editorial Services Coordinator:
Jen Blaney

Interior Layout Tech:
Bill Hartman

Cover Designer:
Mike Tanamachi

Indexer:
Kelly Talbot

Proofreader:
Sandi Wilson

For product information and technology assistance, contact us at **Cengage Learning Customer & Sales Support, 1-800-354-9706**

For permission to use material from this text or product, submit all requests online at **cengage.com/permissions**
Further permissions questions can be e-mailed to **permissionrequest@cengage.com**.

All trademarks are the property of their respective owners.

Library of Congress Control Number: 2009933311

ISBN-13: 978-1-4354-5442-2

ISBN-10: 1-4354-5442-1

Course Technology, a part of Cengage Learning
20 Channel Center Street
Boston, MA 02210
USA

Cengage Learning is a leading provider of customized learning solutions with office locations around the globe, including Singapore, the United Kingdom, Australia, Mexico, Brazil, and Japan. Locate your local office at: **international.cengage.com/region**.

Cengage Learning products are represented in Canada by Nelson Education, Ltd.

For your lifelong learning solutions, visit **courseptr.com**.

Visit our corporate Web site at **cengage.com**.

Printed in Canada
1 2 3 4 5 6 7 11 10 09

To Lourdes, Daniel, and Hannah

Acknowledgments

I would like to thank the many people who made it possible to bring this project together. Thanks to the folks at Cengage Learning, including Mitzi Koontz, for bringing together the idea and the *90 Days* concept. It was a pleasure to work with Cathleen Small in the editing process. Furthermore, I would like to give my sincere thanks to those who invested in me early in my career and began making possible the experiences I share here. Many thanks to Jon Rubin and Peter Costigan. My clients are my lifeblood. Without them, there is no consulting. Special thanks to John Whitehead, John Gideon, Dale Danilewitz, Carol Wood, Louie Torres, Casey Lau, Michael Furlow, Victor Dudemaine, Tom Lyons, Daniel King, Trenton Cycholl, Steve Westmoreland, Glenn Schentag, and Roger Barker for believing in me. There may be no finer profession than consulting if you look at the people in it and around it. To Jill Dyche, Claudia Imhoff, Colin White, Scott Humphrey, Wayne Eckerson, TDWI, Shawn Rogers, Ron Powell, Joe Caserta, Kevin McManus, *Information Management* magazine, SearchDataManagement, Kim Dossey, and Kim Stanick, thank you for being a pleasure to work with. And finally, I could never have done anything if I didn't surround myself with the best. I've had the privilege of working with Charles McCarthy, Afonso da Silva, Cory Shouse, Jeanine Davis, and Stuart Mullins.

About the Author

William McKnight is president of McKnight Consulting Group (www.williammcknight.com). He is one of the leading experts in the information management space and provides services in business intelligence, master data management, data warehousing, and information technology assessment. He has worked with more than 100 corporate clients worldwide. His team's implementations have been recognized with several Best Practices awards.

In addition, McKnight has held executive roles in public and boutique consultancies. He relates to each level of consulting growth and is a passionate communicator and motivator. He is also a former information technology vice president of a Fortune company and holds an MBA from Santa Clara University.

McKnight is a popular keynote presenter at major conferences internationally and has given more than 150 public seminars and webinars. He has hundreds of articles, white papers, and tips in publication. He is widely quoted in the press and was honored as an Ernst & Young Entrepreneur of the Year finalist.

McKnight writes pragmatically from his experience starting from scratch and growing a consulting company, McKnight Associates, Inc., to placement on the Inc. 500 and the Dallas 100 for growth and later selling it as a multimillion-dollar consulting firm.

Contents

Part I: Breaking into Consulting as a Profession

Part II: Establishing and Expanding the Practice

Chapter 4
The Bottom Line 45

Chapter 5
How to Stay Current: Technology and Skills 57

Chapter 6
Service Planning 67

Chapter 10
Acquiring People 115

Chapter 11
Requests for Information/Requests for
Proposals 127

Chapter 12
Client Communications 137

Chapter 13
Writing and Speaking. 147

Part III: Beyond Initial Success

Chapter 17
Marketable Value and Exit Strategies **199**

Chapter 18
Parting Words **211**

Index. **223**

Introduction

In college, when I was working my first consulting job, a professor called with a problem with a slow computer. He had tried everything he knew to fix the problem, to no avail. The computer used to have good performance, but something had happened. Upon arriving at his office, it didn't take me long to spot the problem. There it was: A big red Turbo button—useful in the Off position for some gaming, which he wasn't doing—was begging me to press it. I did. Performance came back. We joked about the $5 payment—5 cents for pushing the button and $4.95 for knowing which button to push.

Good consultants tend to see answers that others don't. *90 Days to Success in Consulting* will aid any consultant or would-be consultant in putting the "business" around the insights and expertise you offer.

Motivations to enter consulting are plenty. Sometimes it's the monetary rewards. Sometimes it's the satisfaction or the control. I'm continually surprised at how many people want to get into consulting. However, there's a lack of solid information about the consulting business. I have something to offer there. *90 Days to Success in Consulting* will help you do consulting right if you really want to get beyond just talk. I try to learn as much as possible every day. I've made more mistakes than I care to remember, but usually not the same one twice. I see mistakes. I've picked up street smarts. All of the information herein is intended as practical knowledge.

The book is organized into three parts, designed to logically take you through the major topics that will be interesting to you at each phase of your consulting journey. In Part I, I cover topics of instantiating the business, including preparing your mind. In Part II, I take you through all the issues required to expand a practice. Part III covers issues in a maturing practice.

I organized the book to be modular, so you can dive into any chapter when you wish to learn about that topic. I did have to reference other chapters occasionally, though. And although you can read the chapters as they interest you, the book is ultimately designed to be read from start to finish and to provide both contextual information and specific deliverables to you in all the topics.

Those specific deliverables are summarized at the end of each chapter in the Action Plan. For those of you who are reading the book before you've started consulting, these are the deliverables to do in the first 90 days after you've thrown down the gauntlet. I anticipate that many of you will have already started consulting. Make the Action Plan items that you haven't done your action plan for the next 90 days. Taken in the aggregate, all of the Action Plan items in the book comprise your work plan for 90 days.

In terms of fields of application of consulting, this book is about the business of consulting and applies to all fields. All consulting has clients, contracts, finances, fees, consultants, employees, proposals, campaigns, outlets for your creativity, and so on. It doesn't matter whether your field of application is information technology—as mine is—marketing, mergers and acquisitions, website design, or workplace safety. Of course, you need to know all about your field (and I give you tips about this in Chapter 5) as well as the business of consulting.

Consulting is such a broad term. There are so many paths within the field. Many are valid. I acknowledge that with this book. I help each consultant design his or her practice. I don't assume you start with immense popularity in your field, a bestselling book, C-level connections, or the skills to mesmerize an audience of thousands at a convention. I won't let you sell yourself short, but you don't have to be any of these to be successful in consulting.

Because independent practitioners and small consulting business owners have some needs that employees of consulting firms don't have, there are a couple of chapters and some other errata that deal with those challenges specifically. Chapter 3 (on the building blocks of the business), Chapter 17 (on exit strategies), and the part of Chapter 15 that deals with partnership business formation may be less interesting to employee consultants at this point in their journey because, depending on your level, many items may be taken care of for you at the firm. However, I have found in 15 years of consulting that the closer you are to running your employee consulting ship like a business, regardless of your role, the higher you will go. Remember, somebody's dealing with all of these issues at every consultancy.

Although I put a gross income goal out there of $500,000 annually, this is decidedly not a get-rich-quick approach. And there's nothing wrong with motivation, but I'm giving you the good, the bad, and the ugly about consulting. It is also not an approach where you leave scorched earth behind you. This approach is about creating a win-win with clients, partners, and staff. It's about knowing when to sell consulting, not just how to sell it. It's about creating a tangible return on investment for your clients, leaving them better off for having engaged your service in the first place. It's a confident but not aggressive or egotistical approach, where your capabilities are what give you your confidence.

It's my distinct pleasure to share with you some of this journey I've been on and the things I've learned along the way. I hope that my advice helps you succeed in whatever aspect of consulting you commit to. Please enjoy. We are all consultants.

Breaking into Consulting as a Profession

Chapter 1

What Is Consulting?

- Who Is a Consultant?
- The Goal: Becoming a Top Consultant
- Consulting in Hard Times
- For Those Entering Consulting Post-Recession
- Client Value-Add
- Action Plan

This book is designed to show you how to leverage your expertise and passion into a lucrative, rewarding career as a consultant.

Like the doctors and lawyers of 30 years ago, consultants are now some of the most respected professionals. However, unlike doctors and lawyers, as well as accountants, builders, and hairstylists, consultants do not require any accreditations. Indeed, there are no diplomas required. Perhaps no self-proclaimed professional designation defies a unique understanding as does consulting. It can mean:

- Looking for first client opportunity
- Independent, on a first or second technical contract
- Independent, established as a technical contractor
- Technical contractor with other technical contractors subcontracted
- Independent consultant
- Independent consultant with other technical contactors subcontracted
- Owner of a consulting firm
- Owner of a consulting firm with market value

It can also mean:

- Contractor employed at a consulting company
- Consultant employed at a consulting company
- Practice leader at a consulting company

A contractor and a consultant are not the same position.

Additionally, there is the "out of work, not interested in working, but giving an air of professionalism in case a plum assignment arises" self-proclaimed consultant.

Note the subtle, but deliberate, transition from contractor to consultant on the ladder. A contractor is someone whose engagements tend to extend client capabilities with hard-to-find technical expertise the client would rather not employ. These engagements are typically arranged by the client because either:

- The skills required are difficult to obtain in anyone who would accept employment
- The skills are only temporarily required

A consultant is required because:

- A client doesn't know enough about something
- A client doesn't know what to do next

In other words, a contractor's job is well specified by the client. The execution steps are understood by the client and those steps are expected to be followed by the contractor. A consultant's job is left to the processes and experiences of the consultant. Perhaps only the high level objectives are communicated. The steps to achieve the goal(s) are not well understood by the client so they are expecting the consultant to bring that to the table. The consultant brings the processes necessary to accomplish the objectives to the relationship. As a result, consultant rates are higher.

These definitions are not uniformly used, but a matter of opinion. Because wherever you are, I want you to progress as high as you desire on this ladder, I will refer to all levels as consultants, but keep in mind that I believe you really have to earn that badge. I progressed through the eight definitions in this order in the seven years with my prior firm, McKnight Associates, Inc. It was a similar progression to that of many other top-echelon consultants who I network with.

Who Is a Consultant?

Perhaps you are a retiree interested in parlaying your years of experience into some part-time income during your retirement years. Perhaps you are on H1B[1], about to get your Green Card[2], and finally free to seek your maximum earning potential. You could be in your twenties and want to get started and really go for it. Or you could be in your thirties or forties and see that you could make double your income by going into consulting. Or perhaps you have other things in your life, and you wish to spend less time to earn the same amount as you are now.

Regardless of who you are or where you are in your consulting path, this book is designed to help you embrace the consulting profession fully and achieve the maximum level possible in the shortest amount of time. Consulting need not be merely a stopgap. It is a well-regarded profession, providing earning power

---

[1]Non-immigrant visa
[2]United States permanent resident card

equal to or greater than almost any other profession and an exciting, stimulating lifestyle. I'll start at ground zero, and I will take you all the way to the top of the ladder—owner of a consulting firm with market value—but I will take it one step at a time. You don't need to be overwhelmed, but I believe you do need to be aware of the profile of the rung you are on as well as the next rung. Aiming all facets of your business at that next rung will actually make it simpler to achieve results right where you are.

Consulting professionals can earn as much as or more than almost any other professionals.

Part I of this book will discuss those foundational activities that you need for your practice. Even those with part-time interests in consulting should adhere to the advisement there. Part II picks up on topics of interest once you have established that you can make money doing this and are ready to take it to another level of professionalism and income. Part III will take you through interesting topics for moving beyond initial success and into advanced levels of success and highly leveraged income. Naturally, all the topics of this book are interesting at all levels of a practice, and I highly encourage you to read them all, regardless of where you feel ready to plateau.

FOR CONSULTANTS EMPLOYED AT CONSULTING FIRMS

Except for some business formation aspects and exit strategies, this book is entirely applicable to those consultants who are employed by a consulting firm and perhaps not interested in owning the firm. Such consultants would be well advised to still direct their activities in a manner almost equivalent to having their own firm. Selling, marketing, staffing, and delivery are applicable to these consultants, especially those near or at the partner level in such firms. Top firms provide some measure of security, as well as a strong incentive bonus plan and rewards sometimes at or near the rewards of the firm ownership path.

The Goal: Becoming a Top Consultant

An annual gross income of $500,000 as a consultant is a very achievable goal. In 90 days, assuming you are starting from scratch, you can be on the path. This does not mean you will necessarily achieve $125,000 in gross income in the next 90 days.

However, you should be into the black with a low-overhead business and establishing the mental, organizational, and other foundational constructs necessary to support a $500,000 gross-income business.

Generating high client value, resulting in $500,000 gross income will be the goal.

The journey is never linear. You have to enjoy the journey, and truth be told, that's all it is—a journey. Let's have a destination while also being open to the fact that the destination could change. It is very important to note that the destination can come in many various forms. As you review the profiles, consider your biases about consulting and the other possibilities as well.

Profile 1 shows the profile of someone who is developing a true consulting practice. It's someone who has branded his practice beyond himself personally, keeps himself pretty active in positions of knowledge leadership, and consequently commands high personal fees.

Profile 1: John Multicapable

Personal billings to end clients	$100,000
White-paper fees and speaking fees	$50,000
Gross margin from external consultant billings	$150,000
Gross margin from employee billings	$200,000
Total	$500,000

Profile 2 shows someone who is, as the vernacular goes, a guru in her industry. She is not pursuing having employees, yet she occasionally reaches out to her network to pull in someone who can fill a job when she cannot. She may not be extremely comfortable with doing that. She is very willing to travel to keep her billings up, and she probably travels 75 percent of the time. The person with this profile will reach this level of income primarily through being a well-known name and giving high-fee seminars.

Profile 2: Jane Guru

Personal billings to end clients	$200,000
White-paper fees and speaking fees	$250,000
Gross margin from external consultant billings	$50,000
Total	$500,000

> **NOTE**
>
> Percent of time traveling will be a constant reference in this book, and it refers to the number of days away from a home base divided by billable days. Due to monthly variations, I refer to this on an annual basis.

Profile 3 shows the profile of a person who has stopped all personal billing, though chances are he did some personal billing at one time. He is making his money from the "spread" (difference between bill rate and pay rate) on other people—employees and outside consultants. His best asset, by far, is the perception of the quality of the people he has at his disposal. It's quite possible that this person is aligned with a vendor or two and specializes in consultants with skills in those vendor products.

Profile 3: David Others

Gross margin from external consultant billings	$250,000
Gross margin from employee billings	$250,000
Total	$500,000

Profile 4 is also the profile of one who does little to no personal billing. This person tracks a network of independent (external) consultants and has a strong recruiting capability. Her business model is to get requisitions from clients and go to her network or go to market to look for those consultants. It's a numbers game, a tough game, with opportunities slipping due to the time it takes to do the search, but some do it quite well.

Profile 4: Jodi Broker

Gross margin from external consultant billings	$500,000
Total	$500,000

Which profile of consulting is best? Conveniently, I've shown them all reaping $500,000 in annual gross income. It's true that any of the profiles can do that (and more) over the duration of a career. It's also true that the $500,000 from Profile 1 has the same spending power as the $500,000 from Profile 2, Profile 3, and Profile 4. Consulting is flexible in this way.

Note that I did not bother yet to get into the post-gross-income expenses of consulting. While the amounts and the makeup of those expenses would differ across the profiles, it is not necessary to spend significant sums on the expense of the consulting business. We will review expenses throughout the book but will focus on it in Part II, when expenses become more significant and are used strategically to expand the practice.

Focus primarily on consulting income, not expenses, in your plan.

Consulting in Hard Times

There is an 800-pound gorilla in the room in every discussion of business during a recession—and that *is* the recession. Periods like the recession that began in 2007 serve as non-gentle reminders about the realities of work and life. With a high unemployment rate, U.S. corporations have had the chisel, not the nailfile, out on their workforce for the last several years. It is not difficult to see the rationale for the reductions, either.

NOTE

On December 1, 2008, we got the official word from the National Bureau of Economic Research that the U.S. economy had been in a recession since December 2007!

Motivated to simply get mortgages out the door, financial institutions lowered and lowered standards. Agents pushed paper in the market, knowing full well that many of the loans had little chance of being repaid. The financial institutions were not motivated to receive payments on the mortgages. They sold and resold the mortgages for present values that approximated full payment—in other words, letting someone else "hold the bag." However, many of the buying institutions were the selling institutions!

Consumers were all too happy to be co-conspirators in the recession. With the ease of obtaining mortgages in the market, real estate prices went up unnaturally, and many were not content to let that equity sit still. Once the unraveling escalated, the terms *negative equity*, *underwater*, and *foreclosure* became front and center in our national dialog.

Spending and lending took grave hits. When spending is down, production is down, and so are jobs. It's a vicious cycle.

Economic recessions may create exceptional opportunities for consultants in the market.

This recession is going to change the way business behaves on many fronts. I believe it is going to tip the scales toward the consulting profession, and there will be unprecedented opportunity for consultants to utilize their skills to establish their value proposition to the market.

As the economy comes back to life, employers are not going to be in any rush to reinstate their permanent workforce. In many respects, they have trimmed the fat from their organization and will view mass hiring as a reintroduction of expenses they do not want to get back into. America is not like some European countries where it is extremely tough to sever an employee relationship, but employees still do tend to, for many reasons, stick around longer than those not in a W2 relationship with the company.

Employers' caution will not obviate the need to ramp up production of goods once again, but rather than create a permanent expense structure with employees, they will seek more freedom with the use of a temporary workforce. According to a March 2009, Associated Press article entitled "How Will We Know When Economy Hits Bottom," "When business conditions improve, employers hire temporary workers first…. [Economist Sophia] Koropeckyj estimated that could come in mid-2010."

Now, don't get me wrong. The consultant I am training you to become is not at all synonymous with "temporary workforce." You do not need this book to become a temporary worker. The point is that mentality will cross into all areas of the business, including those that provide the platform to the goal of $500,000 annual gross income.

Some companies have done a good job in paring their workforce appropriate to the times. Others have cut too many, and many have cut essential elements of their concept to the bone or completely out. Regardless, they will still be reluctant to rehire! This creates opportunities for consultants, and although this book has timeless advice, recession and post-recession are great times to be a consultant. As I write this in the thick of the recession, there is no drop-off in business, I can tell you that.

You may see being a consultant as your *only* option at this point. It doesn't matter. All profiles need to make the most of their talents, and for those in the "no options" camp, I suggest you open up to the possibility that consulting may be more than just a stopgap to a full-time job.

For Those Entering Consulting Post-Recession

Another aspect of the recession worth mentioning is that success hides a multitude of sins. Many corporate sins are now exposed. They need help dealing with that. They are going to be more open to suggestion than ever before. That is where consulting comes in.

The recession has also taught us a thing or two about ethics and our ability, as a massive number of people sharing a planet, to do the "intended" thing. There are many examples of how rules and laws grow over time within an event, company, or country. (For a good one, see Chapter 10 of "The Mind of the Market" [Times Books, 2007] by Michael Shermer.) We're going to see an explosion of regulations designed to keep us out of our next recession. The Sarbanes-Oxley Act of 2002 was enacted in response to a number of major corporate and accounting scandals, and, in my opinion, although it is not cheap to conform to, it has been somewhat effective. Look for more like this. The recession is bringing us new realities that corporations will need help conforming to.

As ethics has taken a hit in the macro environment, it has also taken a hit in the micro environment. Personal credibility and objectivity have always been absolutely necessary for success in consulting, but this is true now more than ever. Can you deliver advisement that is completely in the best interests of your client? Or are you carrying about a bias toward a vendor's products, old ways of doing things, or pre-recession "good times" when return-on-investment (ROI) wasn't asked for (though it should have been)?

Any economic condition is a consulting opportunity.

There is a movement afoot towards only doing those business activities with tangible value to the company. This will include the return of ROI measurements for what we do. This has happened before and will be nothing new to industry veterans who remember 2001 and 2002, when good economic times burst with the dot-com bubble and world events.

Almost instantly vaporized were the speculative, technology-first projects, replaced with a return to the cold, hard question of "Why are we doing this?" With some confidence returning in 2003, some of the handcuffs were loosened. However, the business climate has never returned to pre-2001 glory, and that is a good thing.

Any time a discipline gets too self-absorbed and fails to remember that its long-term existence depends on contribution to the bottom line of the business, it is set up to fail. However, with refocusing the consulting come the challenges. Then and now, consulting, when not inextricably tied to its business results, loses its way within an organization. The value of the underlying infrastructure, processes, and people tends to get overlooked, and the role of consulting in the value chain can be lost.

Ultimately, consulting is more important than it has been for quite some time. The successful techniques that will emerge are those that play to perceived value, and the easiest form of that is reducing company expenses. Whatever the method, consulting must provide perceived and recognized value.

Fortunately, I was exposed to the ROI requirement in my first consulting project, thought it to be a great idea even when not required, and include it routinely now. You should, too.

Client Value-Add

While this book will cover the "blocking and tackling" of the consulting profession, it is important not to lose sight of the prime mover when it comes to consulting success: your ability to delight the customer. Put another way, you need to be value-added to the client. How do you add value? Simply put, the client perceives they received more value than they paid.

Where it is applicable, you should absolutely use ROI to demonstrate the value added of your activity with the client. This is done ideally as a justification for the activity, and then after the fact as a measurement of the activity. Let me explain.

ROI is about accumulating all monetary returns and investments from an activity through to the ultimate desired results—all while considering the possible outcomes and their likelihood. Using ROI for justification is reducing the proposed net change in activities to their associated anticipated cash flow. Often, a cost of money is used to reflect in today's numbers the present value of expected cashflows in the future.

Various ROIs can be computed for the justification of an anticipated project, showing the various potential outcomes distributed across their probability of occurrence—a probability distribution for the project. A probability distribution will use multiple ROI calculations and their likelihood of occurrence to come up with an overall ROI for justification

Mathematical ROI is not possible or relevant for all activities, but ROI as a mindset should be carried into every client situation.

Generate return-on-investment for your clients.

Consider Acme Speakers, a hypothetical prospect for your consulting services. Acme is cash-strapped, like many companies, and does not have money to throw away—as they are willing to tell you (and as you should always assume). They are considering adding Radio Frequency Identification (RFID) tags to their high-ticket items in stores to reduce theft, reduce the time it takes to take inventory, and get closer to just-in-time replenishment of their products. Your firm provides the consulting services they need.

As a high-value consultant, you will be helping them decide whether to adopt RFID. You will use ROI to show how RFID:

- Reduces theft. This is measured by a reduction in anticipated theft over the next three years.

- Reduces the time it takes to take inventory, thereby either reducing the client's employee or contractor costs or freeing up employees to do more value-added activities. Regardless, you measure the value by cost reduction.

- Reduces the cost of inventory. This is a little trickier than the others, but it possibly improves sales by ensuring that items are available that customers want. There is also the possibility of a reduction in space required to store inventory.

The ROI calculation for the project could look something like Figure 1.1.

ROI Worksheet

Project Name: Acme Speakers RFID Project

Cost Reduction		Quarter 1	Quarter 2	Quarter 3
Fraud		$ -	$ 150,000	$ 150,000
	Total Return	$ -	$ 150,000	$ 150,000

Costs to Implement		Quarter 1	Quarter 2	Quarter 3
Curly		$ 75,000	$ 10,000	$ 10,000
Moe		$ 100,000	$ 20,000	$ 20,000
Larry		$ 25,000	$ 10,000	$ 10,000
	Total Investment	$ 200,000	$ 40,000	$ 40,000

| | Net Cash Flow | $ (200,000) | $ 110,000 | $ 110,000 |

ROI Calculations	Quarter 1	Quarter 2	Quarter 3
ROI	0%	55%	110%
Payback Period	$ (200,000)	$ (90,000)	$ 20,000

Figure 1.1
ROI calculation for Acme Speakers RFID project.

For simplicity, Figure 1.1 only considers the first benefit—fraud reduction. Fraud reduction shows as a cost reduction for Acme Speakers. Other categories of return could be for revenue increase and labor savings. Costs to implement are the costs for the three consultants you propose—Curly, Moe, and Larry. Other costs for hardware and software are ignored for now, but in reality, you would want to capture all client costs in the worksheet—those that are paid to your firm as well as to other vendors. (More on service planning in Chapter 6 and partnerships in Chapter 15.) We're also ignoring client employee labor costs (again, for simplicity), but they could also be included.

We are anticipating no fraud reduction in Quarter 1 and $150,000 worth of fraud reduction in both Quarters 2 and 3. We are anticipating a total of $200,000 in costs in Quarter 1 and $40,000 in Quarters 2 and 3.

After returns and costs are reduced to cashflow by quarter, the cashflow is fed into the ROI calculations. Then, the math takes over.

The payback period is the simplest calculation and expresses the point in time at which the overall cashflow from the project turns positive. In this case, the project costs $200,000 in Quarter 1, but there is a net cashflow in Quarters 2 and 3 of $110,000 ($150,000 in returns minus $40,000 in costs). This means at some point in the third quarter, the client will be "in the black" on this project. The client must be willing to be in a net-negative position for two quarters to take on the project.

You may notice that the ROI calculations [(Returns – Costs)/ Costs, using the discount rate to equate dollars to present values] look better and better as time goes on. That's normal. So should you run these calculations out 10 years or so in order to get a hugely positive ROI? No, sorry—the project had better be more than paying for itself in the first year. Chief financial officers, the people who oversee these things, will generally only allow three years at the most in such calculations.

A discount rate is factored into the ROI calculations, but there's no need to get too hung up on that now. As a matter of fact, you may hear the terms *Net Present Value (NPV)* and *Internal Rate of Return (IRR)*. These are equivalent concepts to ROI and utilize

TRUE RETURN ON INVESTMENT CONSIDERS THE DISCOUNT RATE

The ROI calculations use a discount rate of 5% (not shown in the figure), which is the client's "cost of money." Consider if a guy named Eric were to offer you $100 today or $125 in one year. Assuming Eric is good for it, you would take the $125 in one year. (It's 25% interest.) At some point ($110? $108? $105? $102?), you would lose interest in Eric's interest, take the $100, and invest it yourself. Everybody's point will be a little different. The same is true for companies. That breakpoint is called the company's *discount rate*.

the same cashflow and discount rate. Net Present Value (NPV) is the equivalent of what the cashflow stream would be if reduced to a single amount.

If the client already knows the benefits of the RFID project but is seeking qualified consultants to do the implementation, and the selection process is competitive, you will want to think in terms of a concept tangential to ROI called *total cost of ownership (TCO)*. A TCO approach to solution-making is done with an eye to the client's pocketbook. However, costs are seldom simply the implementation costs. There are long-term costs for staff training, support, maintenance, and upgrades. There are also potentially significant costs in integrating the product in with other client infrastructure.

ROI (all forms) will have its place, but the point of demonstrating it now is not because you are going to step into every client situation with the spreadsheet. It's the *mentality of ROI* that you need to adopt to be successful. Many—perhaps most—of your client engagements will not involve doing the ROI math, but they will most assuredly involve generating value-added ROI to your client. By taking this approach to your engagements, you will be highly valued by your clients and generate references and repeat business. Produce ROI for your client, and you will be able to do all the things in this book. Don't do it, and it will be at high peril to your consultancy.

Action Plan

✓ Review the profiles and determine which profile fits your idea of consulting and your skillset and which you will target.

✓ Understand return on investment enough to perform the following payback period calculations in your head (answers at the bottom of the page):

1. Investment of $25,000 in Quarter 1; client's net sales improve by $25,000 in Quarter 2.

2. Investment of $100,000 in the first six months, during which time the client's inventory costs are reduced by $50,000. Inventory cost reduction continues at $20,000 per month.

3. Investment of $1,000,000 in Year 1 and $250,000 per year thereafter for maintenance; client benefits begin in Year 2 at $750,000 per year.

Answers: 1. Quarter 2; 2. Month 9; 3. Year 3

Chapter 2

The Traits of a Professional Consultant

- The Right Frame of Mind
- Clearing Your Life Deck
- Traits of a Good Consultant
- Time Management
- The Consultant Image
- Health
- Travel
- Action Plan

Some of the most important traits for success in consulting are different from what you may think. When I entered the consulting profession, I came from corporate life. I had developed excellent technical skills, which got my foot in the door. I thought those skills would propel me forward as a consultant. And, though they are useful and necessary to success, I learned there were some other skills I had only begun to learn that would enable sustained success.

The Right Frame of Mind

There are so many activities to tend to as a consultant with high aspirations in the profession, including dealing with client pressures, handling the expectation to know more information than those clients, securing the next client, resourcing consultants, forming partnerships, marketing, writing, speaking, and so on. If you need a profession to help you go schizophrenic, consulting may just be the thing for you. However, I am going to give you the first guiding principle of consulting to help you with the prioritization.

To be a top-echelon consultant, you first need to be comfortable earning a living as a consultant. This comfort comes from actually making that living as a consultant—that is, making money. You do your consulting career no favors by having extended periods of non-billing, which create frustration with the profession's ability to ultimately deliver the revenue you desire. More importantly, that doesn't help pay the house bills[1]. Priority one has to be making money. Priorities two and beyond, whatever they may be, fill the non-earning time allocation to the profession and set up your future ability to make money.

A healthy bottom-line business is good for all. You also do your clients no favors by not having a healthy bottom-line business. If the business is not providing more money after expenses than you can make elsewhere, you will fall back into a corporate position that will satisfy those needs, and you will not be there for your repeat business with your clients or get to the high earning potential of consulting. I don't prefer to dwell on the downside. Let's do it right the first time, make money, and make consulting into your career and lifestyle.

---

[1] Or justify your salary at a consultancy if you happen to be employed by one.

Top-echelon consulting is not a profession that is well-served by multimillion-dollar investments and year-plus returns. It's a "now" business. It's a cashflow business. While I will encourage you specifically to measure your finances monthly, the first key performance indicators (KPIs) for your success will be your quarterly income statement. Quarterly gives you enough time to smooth over the inevitable occasional down weeks.

Clearing Your Life Deck

A top consultant is a master of his time. In general terms, his time is dedicated to:

1. Earning money, in both the short and the long term, with consulting.
2. Having fun doing the things he enjoys.
3. Doing that which is not fun but that needs to be done.

Hopefully #1 is fun also. I have tremendous fun consulting. The people I've met as a top-echelon consultant have contributed immensely to the fun in my life. However, to be sure, becoming a top-echelon consultant is hard work. A spectacular resume, top-notch skills, and a network that can be counted on to vouch for you don't come easily. There are more fun things to do than some aspects of consulting.

It's important to minimize option #3—those items that don't contribute to fun or career growth. If you know how to use your time wisely toward consulting career growth, it will be very worthwhile to free up your time to apply to these activities. I call it *adding to efficiency*. However, if you are unwise and unknowledgeable about how to grow with consulting, it really does not matter how much time you free up for misguided notions—you are *adding to inefficiency*.

> Consulting can be tremendous fun.

Though they can all be overcome, having these in your life during your consulting career will be time-suckers, so try to minimize them:

- Travel-averseness. I'll give you some tips on dealing with family when traveling later, in the "Travel" section of this chapter.
- An unorganized home environment. Chaos at home will be a mental drain.

- An unorganized personal financial environment. Ditto the mental drain aspect, but also, personal finance issues can tend to take precedence over the finances of the business.

- Golfing. You do need to exercise and stay fit for consulting, but golfing is not the most compacted-exercise sport. Still, if you are good at it already, do keep it up, and you can use it to your advantage. If you don't play or you're terrible at it, the effort required to get good at it can be better spent on other things. Excuse yourself from business golf outings if you are a triple-bogey player.

In general, you want to make the non-fun part of your homelife as "lights out" as possible, even to the point of not requiring you to do much except some provide some oversight for things to hum along. Read Timothy Ferriss' excellent book *The 4-Hour Workweek* (Crown, 2007) for some tips in this department.[2]

Traits of a Good Consultant

A sense of urgency is required to become a top consultant. No one becomes a top consultant by being lucky. If you want to progress rapidly, you need to go after it every day. Wasted days, months, or years can be grave to the career.

Being a realist with optimistic leanings is best. I have seen blind optimism inhibit course correction while the practice goes down the drain in the process. The KPIs, the pure numbers of this business, don't lie. As I expose them to you in the course of this book, take them to heart, at face value. For high achievement in consulting, you cannot be a pessimist.

All kinds of backgrounds and personalities make it in consulting.

You might think I would suggest that a huge ego is best in becoming a top consultant. Actually, I don't want to single out a personality type in this department as best for consulting. Top consultants come in all personality types. There is an opinion that, when starting out, one should keep the ego in check. On the other hand, it works for some people to create that air of expertise early and "fake it until you make it." My take is that you must be confident in order to be successful. But that confidence comes

---

[2]Although I love Tim Ferriss's book, the concept, and the advice to "work myself out of a job," which is essentially the message of the book, it is *not* the manual for becoming a top consultant.

from true knowledge and ability, not from empty bragging. And no one likes someone who is overtly or subtly always trying to put themselves one up in a situation.

Goal orientation is also high on the list. Complacency has no place in a top consultant career.

And frankly, it doesn't matter if you were raised dirt poor or with a silver spoon in your mouth. My lot was the former, which I think made me act hungry and desperate in order to never return to that state. People from the other side of the tracks can tend to have a comfort level with success and an expectation level. Sometimes their connections can be of help. As you'll find out, this is a people business. However, you can, with effort, quickly build up your network regardless of where you start out. Either profile can work as long as complacency is not part of the equation.

Technical skills are much more commonplace and more easily acquired than good communication skills. You need both to be a top consultant. I would cite communication as much higher than my technical skills in what helped me get to be a top consultant. I've spent copious time communicating with upper management at clients who may or not be extremely technical. I've spent equal time crafting communication for them. There are numerous consultants who have higher technical skills than I, but who have earned far less because they didn't apply the techniques in this book to their practice. Good communication skills come naturally to some, but they can also be learned. I will focus on how to grow these skills in Chapter 13, "Writing and Speaking," but, to be sure, they are needed in all pre-delivery, delivery, and post-delivery functions of being a top consultant.

Time Management

Ironically, as you grow your practice, you will probably have more time to work without obvious tasks to be done than at the beginning of your practice. This is because at the beginning, you are the one out there executing the contract. Most consultants cum contractors are in a cycle of contract, time off looking for the next contract, contract, time off looking for the next contract, and so on. This cycle could generate a six-figure income, but it won't make you a top consultant.

Maybe you are thinking that you wish you could get into that pattern! Fine. I wish that for you as well if you are below it, and I will certainly help you get there, but I encourage you to be aware of the higher profiles and shoot for more. Getting beyond it means you do some of the true consulting tasks in this book during the downtime in your contract cycle. This downtime comes not only during nights and weekends, but also during many contracts that are not full time.

> A successful consultant knows he or she is working a business as well as a client.

Working in space (without obvious tasks to complete) means *working* in space. Whether in between contracts, during downtime, or once you establish an income stream with others on billing, there are significant non-billing activities in being a top consultant. As I discuss them in the ensuing chapters and give you their relative priorities, you need to fill your non-personal-billing time with them. This is where you have to be a self-starter. No one will be looking over your shoulder during this time. No one else will care what you do. Give yourself goals and benchmarks related to those activities.

You have to be an opportunist when you're starting out. There were times early on when multiple contract opportunities presented themselves, and I was able to wedge both into my schedule. This left no time for firm building, but the money I raised (and saved) built my cushion so I could tolerate bench time at a later point if it ever came (it never did!) and fund some firm-building activities.

Similarly, after I built my reputation, I was able to leverage it on *inbound* calls (much preferred to outbound calls) and work with clients to provide another person for their requirements who I would mentor and support. As well, I would provide billable hours to the project such that the contract details looked like this:

Consultant	Allocation	Rate
Joe Smith	100%	$125
William McKnight	10%	$250

I could actually work another contract full time (~90 percent) and provide this level of support to this engagement. The actual allocation would vary based on the capability and fit of the consultant to the job. My goal and hope was that it would be close to zero. You may wonder why I would make such a statement. After all, I suggested earlier that you need to optimize your revenue, and this would be bypassing $250 an hour, which, if I'm doing

10 percent, is $1,000 a week or roughly $4,375 a month. That's not going to make or break the firm, but it's good money. Here's why: You need to excel at the *non-personal* billing business to become a personal top consultant. You do not do this by having to tend to every consultant you have out on billing. A strong network initially (and later, the ability to employ) will help ensure fit and the freedom of your time to work on the firm (that is, to get *other* consultants out on billing).

NOTE

Top Consultant = Reputation + Network + Abilities

The Consultant Image

You should look the part as a top consultant or a future top consultant. Your clothing need not be expensive, but it should not appear worn, torn, or stained. It should fit well. You should dress one level up from the level at the client sites you are dealing with.

Even if your clients have casual Friday dress, don't do it. Never wear jeans or sneakers to business sites for sales visits or delivery.

Here are a few other tips for your visual presentation—that important first impression:

- Don't be more than 24 hours from your last shave—and if you have a beard or mustache, keep it trimmed.
- Don't have any visible tattoos.
- Trim your nose and ear hair—alternate these two every time you shave.
- Make sure you don't have anything protruding from your nose!
- No "manbrow"—hit that gap with the razor!
- No belts that show how your waistline has expanded (or contracted) through wear at holes you're not using now. When you change holes, change belts.
- Wear a watch.
- Wear a PDA.
- Wear your wedding ring if you have one. You need "artifacts" or accessories so you don't appear too plain.

- Never be more than 30 to 45 days from your last haircut, and hit the burns around your ears once or twice with the electric razor in between haircuts.
- Zip your zipper.
- Check for food in your teeth after eating *anything*. (But check, pick, and brush in private or in the restroom.)
- Button up your shirt, leaving only the top button undone. This is not a time to show off your hairy chest—or, for ladies, your cleavage. (See the "Sex Appeal" sidebar.)
- Get the sleep gunk out of your eyes.
- Wipe your mouth if there's the slightest chance that the last bite left a residue.
- Use mouthwash in the morning. Teeth brushing is not enough for breath fitness.
- Men should have trimmed fingernails.
- Makeup (ladies): It's "neutral business." Start with a good concealer and foundation, use natural eye shadow and blush, and finish the look with mascara and a neutral lipstick.[3]

SEX APPEAL

Ladies, in their work with men, especially need to be cognizant of whether they are projecting an image that is enticing for the wrong reasons. We all enjoy seeing attractive members of the gender(s) that we're attracted to. And there is nothing wrong with being attractive in a business setting, but always stay professional in your appeal.

Extra credit:

- Use a bronzer occasionally.
- Use a teeth whitener.
- Keep the wrinkles at bay by moisturizing your face once or twice daily.
- Use moisturizer with sunscreen during high sun months.

Consultants earn in the top quartile (25 percent) of Americans. Top consultants earn in the top percentile (1 percent). Look like it. It does inspire confidence. Make sure the consultants who

---

[3]Thanks to Lourdes McKnight for these tips.

work for you subscribe to good habits as well. How would you like a call from a client to tell you that your consultant has gas or smells too bad? I've received those calls, and they set back the client relationship.

You should also sound the part of a top consultant or a future top consultant. Being articulate is important. Remember the need for communication skills mentioned earlier? Use complete sentences when you speak. Eliminate lazy and slang talk (for example, yeah and ain't). No one, from any walk of life, is automatically immune to this.

Be someone clients are comfortable being around.

Speak clearly and appropriately. Your vocabulary should be at a college level.[4] Small talk normally precedes business talk. Be knowledgeable of current events—at least to the point where you can converse about the main points. However, be careful not to make judgmental or assumptive comments of any kind until you know the other person well. She could actually be in favor of the hurricane coming, or that picture on his desk could be his wife, not his daughter. Be careful. Even if you happen to speak in agreement with the person's position or guess the person in the picture on the desk right, the client would know that you just made a lucky guess.

Health

Consulting can be demanding physically at the top consultant level. However, the physical exhaustion actually feels good after winning a deal, satisfying a client, having a breakthrough, or completing an article for publication. If healthy living is part of who you are, it will be helpful to you in your pursuit of top consultant status.

The physical demands are double what they otherwise would be because of the travel. I will give travel tips in the next section, but do know that is partly why you need to be in reasonable shape as a top consultant.

The days as a top consultant can be quite varied. On some days, there will be travel. On other days, there will be sitting at home banging on a keyboard or talking on the phone—sometimes

---

[4]Subscribe to the Very Vocabulary podcast—listen and learn.

doing challenging work, sometimes not. There will be presentations to give and the need to be active and engaged with clients—and alert at all meetings. There will be short and long commutes.

Many aspects of life figure into becoming a top consultant.

To me, this is stimulating. I enjoy the variety of work. Good health helps to sustain the practice. I've seen several promising consultants back away from consulting to take "real" jobs when their health condition no longer permitted them to carry on.

This is not a health book, but the main health points for our purposes are:

1. Keep your weight in line with USDA guidelines.[5]
2. Do cardio that brings up your heart rate to target heart rate levels four times per week.
3. Stretch daily. Wake up slowly, stretching whatever feels like it needs to be stretched. If you don't take up yoga practice, at least touch your toes and stretch out your groin, quadriceps, and back regularly.
4. Firm and tone with resistance exercise three times per week. At the very least, work your chest and arms.
5. Eat five servings of fruits or vegetables every day, with fruit juice being only one of those.
6. Keep to a lowfat diet, avoiding fried foods, extra butter and oil, thick creams and sauces, and desserts.
7. Keep to a moderate alcohol intake.
8. Have ample protein in the diet—and yes, you can get it from nonmeat sources.
9. If you smoke, consider quitting.

Otherwise, blood pressure checks (for example, at drug stores), annual lipid profiles, and a checkup from your doctor should offer up further items to address for your good health. Without good health and the ability to work, and without an employer who is required (or willing and able) to work with your health issues, it could be bad news for the practice. You can learn and implement everything else in this book, but you can't continue if you don't take care of your health. Get and stay healthy—and encourage your family to be healthy, too.

---

[5]www.usda.gov

Travel

Clients will pay top dollar for top-consultant consulting, including travel. They will not pay it for contracting. If you want to be a top consultant, you will do some traveling. The only place in America I can imagine living and still earning close to your maximum in this business without traveling is New York City. And there are definitely numerous places you can live where you will do 80 percent or more travel. Even if you ramp up teams at client sites and pull back personally, you will travel to other client sites to sell and start up new engagements if you live in Eagle, Idaho or Jeffersonville, Indiana.

You need to decide how important staying home is to you. If it is of the utmost importance, and you can't bear to be away from home for more than 20 days per year, then you will not reach top consultant level. Period. You could still enjoy maximizing your earnings with limited time devoted to your work, and consulting may still be the best venue for you. Those consultants who do so for part-time income can be selective about their assignments, and one of the criteria they may apply is travel. For some, this is a desire *to* travel, and for others, it's a desire *not* to travel.

I mentioned the challenges of managing your time as a consultant across the stratification of activities. Now consider that many of those activities will involve travel, and the time-management challenges exacerbate. I don't know how to stress this enough, but while I'm talking about travel planning may be the perfect time to do it: You need to be proactive about the things that matter to you. Prospects and clients will be notoriously unconcerned with the hassle involved in your travel. They may also be unconcerned with your travel costs, especially when you're paying. You will need to raise these issues at the appropriate time in the conversation. If it's a sales call and your presence is requested, the expectation is that you will pick up your costs.

Now, if I were to tell you I've figured out how the airline industry prices their fares, I would be lying. That would take another book and another person, but, as a frequent traveler and one passing along some tips here, I can tell you that there is a correlation between advance booking and fare. Rate hike-up points seem to hover around the three-week and two-week levels.

There will be times when you will have to make a judgment call, bite the bullet, and pay the high fare. If the upside is high enough, and you have the time cycles for it, go for it. However, you need to determine at what point you will introduce your need to plan your time and budget your travel dollars into the equation. This concept applies to all of the (mostly) pre-sales work that you do—when is enough enough? I will delve into that topic later in this book. You must consider the serious commitment of your most valuable asset—time—as well as money to travel to sell an opportunity.

Time is your most valuable asset as a consultant; spend it wisely.

When the client is paying for the travel, occasionally they will give you their travel policy, which outlines what they are willing to pay for various categories. I don't believe I have ever read those policies. Regardless of whether the client is paying for the travel, I spend the money *as if it were my own*. I've never had a personal expense report sent back or short-paid by a client.

When I'm on my own, I do not pay for first class. I do not require five-star hotels. Occasionally, I'll even do a fleabag hotel for a night to save money. I would rather use my time working, exercising, and relaxing, so when I'm alone, I do not do fine dining, and I do not buy wine with meals. If you are not as inclined to be a skinflint as I am, you may have to read those policies and stick to them. Don't expense what is likely to get rejected by the client. And don't nickel and dime the client with your tips, postage, snacks, and so on.

I've had expense reports for my consultants kicked back to me for various reasons over the years. One was nabbed for drinking more than two beers at dinner. Another was for weekend expenses when the consultant was staying over at the client location so there would be one airfare instead of two. The beers incident was easy—eat it. The multi-hundreds for the hotel were not as easy to walk away from, but because it was a long-term customer (and shame on me for not clearing it up beforehand), I did. And so should you.

There will be set-backs in consulting.

This book will not tell you how great you are and that you should set your prices and standards high and never compromise, so that you don't work and you get to retire with your big ego. Keep it in check and prepare to lose a few battles while you keep your eye on winning the war.

Rental car costs have gone through the roof in recent years. For whatever reason, they have become the convenient whipping boy every time a city wants to impose some new taxes. The mentality goes something like, "Our local people live here, so they don't rent cars and hotel rooms here. Those are paid for by those nasty out-of-towners." It makes passing the tax more palatable. Consequently, auto rental (and hotel, to some degree) bills have filled with costly line items that aren't in the rate that the companies quote you. Be aware. As for the high costs of auto rental, consider your options for the transportation you need in the town. Of course, there are taxicabs. Many mid- and large-sized cities have excellent public transportation as well. New York City and Chicago come to mind. Personally, I would never rent a car and deal with the traffic in huge cities. Research the city on the Internet as you plan your trip.

NOTE

Citysearch is a good portal for city information, and Google Earth is an excellent tool for viewing your needed travel pattern within a city.

It will usually be cheaper to take a cab from the airport to the hotel or client (and back again at the end) than to rent a car anyway. And even though it limits my options, I am usually fine with the dining choices at or near the hotel. Plus, you have the bonus of not having to hassle with the car (renting it, parking it, gassing it back up, returning it, and driving in a strange city).

Regardless, at some point, it probably makes sense to own a global positioning system (GPS) or activate that function on your cell phone if it's available. Be sure to get one you can travel with for those trips where you will be renting a car.

Back to hotels... Given my vehicle strategy, I give a lot of preference to those hotels close to the client. Minimize your commute and utilize the time savings elsewhere for the business. Consider that you probably commuted many hours by plane (and to/from airports) just to be there anyway. Many clients have a list of preferred close hotels where they have discounts. Ask about it. These may be the only ones they wish to pay for if their paying is part of the arrangement.

Within that constraint, you may want to cluster your stays in a single chain as much as possible. Marriott, Hilton, and Hyatt have locations all over with a consistent look and feel and good frequent-stay programs. There is also a new breed of hotel forming with fewer of the frills and large, imposing lobbies; more simple conveniences (walk-in kitchens, comfortable open areas to sit, and so on); and lower costs. I highly recommend using them wherever possible. These include AmeriSuites, La Quinta, Candlewood Suites, and Hyatt Express. Most of these are owned by a larger hotel chain, so you still get that chain's frequent-stay points. Sometimes it is hard to determine the most suitable hotel from afar, so when I am traveling and I see a more suitable hotel, I make a note of it in my PDA for the next visit.

One aspect of travel that cannot be overlooked is being away from family and the sheer loneliness factor that accompanies the isolation. Certainly, the goal to become a top consultant is a family decision. Some technology, such as Skype (for no-cost calling), text messaging, email, and webcams can help ensure the business traveler that all is well on the home front as he or she takes care of business.

Consulting is a family decision.

When you return home from a trip, you are likely to be exhausted. The family, on the other hand, has accumulated numerous activities for you upon your return! These may include house chores or other family events. Indeed, a business trip begins before you leave for the airport, and remnants of it continue well after you arrive home. Being prepared personally and with your family can make this aspect a very palatable part of becoming a top consultant.

Action Plan

✓ Discuss the commitment with your spouse or significant other.

✓ Do (or have someone do) an honest check of your image and, if necessary, update your image.

✓ Get a health checkup and adopt healthy practices; you're going to need them.

Chapter 3

The Top Consultant Image Building Blocks

- Business Name
- Logo: The Little Icon That's Supposed to Convey Everything
- Slogan
- Website
- Other Tools of the Trade
- Domiciling Your Business
- Action Plan

In this chapter, I will cover some practical business formation issues. This is often a major education hurdle for owning a business, so I hope to clear up some of the complexity. For those of you consulting within an existing practice, this chapter will be less interesting, but perhaps it will provide some background on how those who founded the company went about it.

Business Name

Naming the business should not be a source of anguish. If you name yours with an extension of your name, as I did (McKnight Associates, Inc. and McKnight Consulting Group), you need not hang your head and mumble your chosen name with embarrassment when you state your name and company if you really are a "one-man band." The methods in this book will help the one-man bands shed this image when desired or make it a non-factor in consultant selection. Many clients will prefer a small firm anyway, and using a last name—regardless of whether you are still small—will allow you to compete. In other words, the name doesn't matter as much as you may think it does.

Let's look at the names of some firms that are primarily consulting firms: Deloitte, Accenture (formerly Anderson), BearingPoint (formerly KPMG), PricewaterhouseCoopers (PWC), and Cap Gemini. All except Cap Gemini were named for the last names (or initials of four last names in the case of KPMG) of real people. Innumerable firms have achieved high status for their founders by being named with last names of the founders. Some have even completely made up last names when their legal last names did not sound right for the business. (Perhaps they were long, difficult to pronounce, humorous, or sent the wrong message, such as Pigg or Ripoffe.)

If you want to change your business name, you can always "dba" (do business as) another name.

If you are going into this with cofounders, the naming should reflect your best guess at which name or names your intended clientele will respond to, leaving egotism aside. If Thornton, Boucher, and Cunningham are going into a consulting business together, and Thornton is the known name and Boucher and Cunningham are not, the choices for the basis of the company name could be:

- Thornton
- Thornton and Boucher (or Thornton and Cunningham)
- Thornton, Boucher, and Cunningham

The advantage of just Thornton is that it is the name people know. However, the firm may have aspirations to create known names out of Boucher and/or Cunningham as well. Basing it on Thornton alone may also alienate Boucher and Cunningham. However, it may be difficult to attract employee number four with such a naming structure unless this firm makes it clear the value that each owner is contributing (and they're stopping at three people at this level). It will also be important for Thornton, Boucher, and Cunningham to gain traction quickly and establish the firm name, making it clear that it would be a difficult rebranding to add other names to the company name.

More partnership issues will be covered in Chapter 15, "Partnerships."

If you take this advice and use a last name, the simple way to go is to append Associates (some will prefer "and Associates") or Consulting (or Enterprises or Group) to it. You will need to do a name search, and the company name should easily translate to its URL. People naturally type www.companyname.com and hope they will find what they're looking for. Some will drop out of the process if they have to look up a business card or do a Google search for you. For example, if you are interested in Gartner Consulting, but the URL gartnerconsulting.com is taken, you have created this multistep problem. It's not necessarily a knockout, though. I had to add a hyphen to a URL (www.mcknight-associates.com) because www.mcknightassociates.com was taken. If you are going to develop a reputation around an individual (a "guru"), try to secure www.firstnamelastname.com of that person and redirect it to your business URL. Yes, I know I am spending time on web marketing during the discussion of business naming, but the two topics are interrelated.

Logo: The Little Icon That's Supposed to Convey Everything

You need a logo. Pick the colors carefully (or have them picked carefully for you), because they should also be used on the website and your stationery (if you have stationery). Unless logo-building is a strength of yours, I suggest spending $200 for a reputable graphic artist who will keep working at it until he or she gets something you approve. In Chapter 14, "Managing Capital,"

I will advise you about which outside services are worth it for a top consultant and which are not.

Here are some example artists for the logo:

- www.logoexpertz.com
- www.logovogue.com

Both of these are based outside the United States. That is not a problem. Utilization of services from countries where the labor is cheaper and quality is high is something well worth getting used to.[1]

Alternatively, you could get Photoshop software and kluge one together yourself. There's so much else to do that I recommend paying and having this done. Either way, get three versions of the logo (see Figure 3.1):

- Base logo
- Base logo (smaller) with the name spelled out
- Base logo (small version) with the name and slogan (see the following section) spelled out

Figure 3.1
*Three versions
of the logo.*

SMART CONSULTING GROUP

LOGISTICS CONSULTING GROUP
Sound and Smart Demand Planning Success

---

[1]This is not a comment on how things "should be" in terms of public policy toward outsourcing.

Slogan

You need a brief, one- to six-word "slogan" that conveys your top competitive advantage or differentiator. It's what you want to be known for. This will go on your webpage, one of your logos, and quite possibly your business card. It will also go on any giveaways that you eventually have made.

The competitive advantage basis for the slogan is well worth thinking through—not just for the slogan, but for your "elevator pitch" that you will use to differentiate your company. Based on *Creating Competitive Advantage: Give Customers a Reason to Choose You Over Your Competitors* (Broadway Business, 2006), an excellent book that I recommend consultants give a full read to, here is a sample list of measurable deliverables that consultants may have over their competition:

- Product knowledge
- Consultant availability
- Personality that is easy to work with
- Full lifecycle knowledge and skills
- Unique lifecycle front-end skills
- Unique lifecycle back-end skills
- Unique business skills that complement the technical skills
- Geographic accessibility
- Fast and accurate response to customers
- Unique design capabilities
- Training capabilities
- Industry knowledge and capabilities
- Unique credibility among consultant(s)

What do you want your firm to be known for? Incorporate that into your slogan and logo.

Visit www.adslogans.co.uk for some ideas on phrasing.

> **NOTE**
> *Lifecycle* refers to the ability to see the project impact from early thought through production and beyond.

Website

You will be updating your website frequently. It needs to be built in a manner in which you can update it quickly and modularly. Whether you build your own website should depend on your website development skills. For the many of you who are website development literate, this may be something you can do yourself. If you are offering web services, you surely should do your own website to deflect the obvious question about why you didn't build your own.

However, there does exist a robust marketplace of consultants who can build your website. Check out www.elance.com or www.homestead.com for some marketplace options, and don't rule out foreign firms that are inexpensive. Check out your prospective vendor thoroughly, but still give yourself enough time for a false start or two. You may even waste some money with a down payment before deciding several weeks into the relationship that it is not going to work out.

The website is very important. It's your virtual face to the world. You need the right vendor and the right system for updates. Don't hesitate to pull the plug if the vendor is not responsive or clearly does not comprehend your direction. This will likely not get much better as time goes on, so get in bed with one you can live with.

> **NOTE**
> Remember this experience! The shoe will be on the other foot when you are soliciting business. How did you like to be treated by your vendor? What did you like? What didn't you like?

The website is important. Take care in building it.

Technology-wise, vendors (and perhaps you, if you build websites) can tend to get locked into certain technology that they are used to. You will have to consider the ability of hosting providers to support the technology that the website is developed in and the support that the vendor behind the technology is going to give it in the future.

Regardless of who builds the site, expect to come up with the content yourself, as well as contribute to the design. If you are using an outside provider, at the least you will want them to present you with three to five design options from which to choose.

Prospects will check out your website as they decide whether to do business with you. They will check it out for quality, and they will check it out for content. If you just told a client that you are a specialist in XYZ, the client can go to the website to see whether you just made that up because it's what they wanted to hear or whether you have a commitment to it in the form of service offerings and intellectual content, such as articles and presentations.

Look for ideas at your competitors' websites—whether the competitor is large or small doesn't matter. From *Content Critical: Gaining Competitive Advantage Through High-Quality Web Content* (FT Press, 2001), McGovern and Norton suggest that readers want seven things when they visit your website:

- To find things
- Your advice
- Up-to-date, quality content
- Relevant and straightforward content
- To do things
- To interact
- Privacy

These sections should just about cover all consultancy website content needs:

- Contact information
- About us
- Service offerings
- Presentation calendar
- Media mentions
- Articles
- Downloads
- Press releases
- Client list
- Partner list

Although you should know how to update the content of your entire website, here are some areas of the website that you will want to update frequently and quickly.

You will not want the overhead of engaging an outside party to do these:

- Presentation calendar
- Web and media mentions of you and your company
- Articles that have been published
- Additional (or updates to existing) professional services offered
- Additional (or updated to existing) training courses offered
- Downloads available to readers
- Press releases
- Client list
- Partner list
- Front-page content you are highlighting, which could include some of the above

The rest of the site will be fairly static, as will be the design.

Your website will have lots of dynamic content. Be change-enabled.

You'll want email addresses for yourself (for example, first initial and last name) as well as info@yourdomain.com. Some top consultants will have more like careers@yourdomain.com, sales@yourdomain.com, resumes@yourdomain.com, and so on. For me, if all the emails are coming to me, I don't want to get carried away with complexity. Even if an email comes into info@yourdomain.com, I suggest responding with your personal email address to make it more personal.

Finally, an important note is that the website should be developed with SEO (search engine optimization) principles in mind and that it is well worth the extra effort to optimize your website for harvesting by the major search engines, such as Google. Basic website SEO tips are easy to find. Try to get your website affiliated with certain keywords that are unique to your practice. If you feel strongly that you would be one of a handful of companies to utilize high-traffic keywords, it may well be worth it to engage an SEO service to ensure the repeated submissions that are necessary to solidify the link between those keywords and your services. Otherwise, paid services for SEO have, in my opinion, dubious value for consultancies.

Other Tools of the Trade

You will need to utilize a title in your practice. I like President. In some bios, I am also Founder and/or Senior Consultant, but I am always President. It does not say I am President of IBM or some large company. It says President of my company/my practice.

I find many consultants shy away from President because it conveys a sense of distance from a client and an awkward moment when suggesting yourself as a resource for the assignment. Hogwash! Small practices are run by actively engaged leadership, and clients know it.

Confidence is important in consulting. If your title makes you uncomfortable to the point that you will be embarrassed by it, pick another one. We'll talk about titles for your expanding practice in Part II of this book, but for now, here are some alternative titles to President:

- Principal
- Executive Vice President
- Partner
- Vice President of _____
- Director

Business cards are important. They should contain your logo, one of your slogans, your address, email, fax, phone, and URL. You can use FedEx Office. If a printer provides a good value proposition for this business, it's likely they will for all (of their kind of) business. Just go with them from now on.

NOTE

Get an 800 fax number from www.eFax.com. You want to create location transparency (you can work from anywhere) and self-sufficiency in your practice. Internet faxing meets these criteria better than dealing with paper. eFax currently offers random area-code fax numbers for a discount. Don't do this.

Speaking of phone: again, simplicity rules. It's easiest to just make your cell number your main number. Some will argue the virtues of web-based calling, such as Skype or Vonage. You can get a web-based number, but a consultant's schedule is inconsistent, and you will not be consistently available at your computer for those inbound web calls. The cell phone gives you more options. Also, when you have office days, if, as is true for most of us, a landline will provide a better sound and connection, you can use landlines (or the web) for *outbound* calls. You can also forward your cell phone opportunistically to your landline for inbounds, but I wouldn't get into giving out multiple numbers. You can block your outbound number with a *69[2] before dialing, but if a prospect gets hold of your home number, that should not be a problem unless there are family concerns. Those old lines you had between work and home are eroding.

Once you get your phone number and email address out there in a public way (on your website, in article bios, and so on), your spam and telemarketing will increase. I have yet to completely solve this problem, and I'm sure I never will. Just learn to deal with it. Some would disagree with this, but as a rule of thumb, I sometimes don't answer the phone unless I know who it is or I'm expecting a call, because so many of the calls are telemarketing. That's the breaks, I guess, when you make your number public.

Consequently, I (and most top consultants) pass *a lot* of information through email and *schedule* most of my substantive phone calls. If those phone calls are going to be with three parties, use a conference calling service, such as www.conferencecall.com or www.gotomeeting.com. Spend a little time locating the best conference call service for you. When the volume of these types of calls gets high enough, it will be worth it to have your own dedicated conference call number.

Finally, as you grow your business, you will need a "pocket folder" with your inserts to leave behind. A pocket folder gives you options to put the targeted inserts in that you need for the situation. Get your logo/slogan engraved on the pocket folder.

> **NOTE**
> Many refer to this type of material as a *leave behind.*

---

[2]Check with your phone company to confirm.

I've never had a need for real stationery, since most communication is carried out over email. It's easy enough with Microsoft Word to create what passes for stationary on a laser-jet printer.

Domiciling Your Business

Do you need outside office space? At very least, you need an outside address for mail—a postal mailbox (PMB) from a Mail Boxes Etc. type of service. I know many top consultants who have used their home address for years with no problems. Indeed, if anybody really wants to find out where you live, it can certainly be done these days. However, I feel more comfortable *not* using my home address for my business. I recommend separating the two.

Using PMBs is not without its problems. First off, they are required to tell you that you "need" to use PMB in the address, and, of course, this would look unprofessional as a business address. However, you should be able to use "Suite" instead, which is much more professional. Furthermore, you need to actually go to the box to get the mail.

Be a business with low overhead. This is the direction that business is going.

As for outside space, I recommend it when you do not have space for a dedicated office in the home. It is difficult and not recommended to use a corner of the bedroom or kitchen. Even if you have the room, if that space is not quiet (or you cannot soundproof an area) from kid or other family noise, you could need space outside the home. As you grow your operation and have staff and the need for frequent meetings with them, you may also need outside space then.

There is also a middle ground that is a good option in your first year or so, until you have the need for staff and a place to have frequent meetings with them, and that is a virtual office. Regus is an example of a worldwide virtual office provider. You can get an allocation of 40 or 20 or some number of hours per month of office space and the use of an address. Be judicious in your commitment to the virtual office infrastructure (utilizing their phone numbers, mail, and fax for inbound) in case it is a short-lived arrangement.

When you need to meet clients, partners, prospects, candidates (employee or contract), vendors, and so on, I have one word for you: Starbucks. Go to any Starbucks during business hours, and you will see people working and business meetings happening.

Other coffee shops are similarly set up. It's not shameful to request your meetings at Starbucks. Just buy a beverage while you're there for the rent.

Action Plan

✓ Name your business

✓ Get a logo designed

✓ Select your title

✓ Determine your slogan

✓ Determine your phone strategy

✓ Get an electronic fax number

✓ Reserve your URL and put up your website

✓ Order your business cards

✓ Sign up with a conference calling service

✓ Determine your business address strategy

Establishing and Expanding the Practice

Chapter 4

The Bottom Line

- Securing Income to Get Started
- Brokers
- Business Formation and Taxation
- Insurance
- Startup Money
- Action Plan

In Chapter 1, I defined a goal of making $500,000 on average per year. I purposely left off all the immeasurable intangibles, such as popularity, interesting trips, and industry impact. Those come along and are nice to have, but really, the initial focus has to be on the bottom line first and foremost. A healthy business is a healthy bottom line. And, frankly, if you were to ask yourself what you want most out of your consulting business, compensation would surely be near the top as either the goal itself or the means to some other ends, such as lifestyle, security, and so on.

So, we need to talk about securing initial income. This guidance applies whether you are at your own firm or you are an employee in a practice at a consulting firm, with the caveat that some firms are going to be less interested than others in some client-sharing concepts, such as using job boards and brokers.

Securing Income to Get Started

Being a consultant is nothing more than utilizing your skills and creativity, as well as having an unburdened nature to generate and capitalize on progressive opportunities.

I strongly recommend that a new consultant secure income while instantiating the business (website, offerings, partnerships, pocket folders, business cards, logos, slogan, and so on). This income can come in the form of working at a regular job or, in a quasi-beginning on the top consultant path, taking a contract. Then, on nights and weekends (and spare days from the job or contract), you can lay down the infrastructure for yourself so that in the future you do not have to:

- Take a contract through a broker (see the following section), which you may have had to do for your first contract
- Have only yourself to sell because you are perceived as a contractor, not a business owner who has resources beyond himself
- Take low rates

Brokers

Brokers are people and companies of varying sizes who are the middleman between the client and the contractor. Client companies find it easier to outsource the function of locating their contractors to these entities as opposed to doing it themselves.

Brokers also generally seek more of a "commodity" type of consultant.[1] The brokers are usually looking for "onesy, twosies"—that is, individuals who are going to fit into a predefined role at the client, not "consultant" individuals who are going to do some role definition for not only themselves, but for others at the client site, employees included. End client companies will generally go to consulting organizations for those.

Brokers are your allies. They are not the enemy. When you are starting out, if they're your best option for maximum rate and you're not established yet to the point of needing your time to work multiple deals, by all means use a broker. You can even observe their practices and how they engage you. In the near future, *you* will be doing the brokering. Recalling the profiles from Chapter 1, you may decide to attain the $500,000 level by leading with brokering services.

> You can make money from brokers in three fundamental ways—working their clients, helping them find the opportunities, and finding the people to fill the deals.

However, most brokers will not be able to comprehend or process dealing with a consultant who will want to insert a person other than himself (and take a bite) into the deal. Practically speaking, that reduces the split. Consider:

- The client is looking to pay $125 per hour.
- The broker is offering to you $87.50 per hour.[2]
- You are offering $75 per hour to your consultant.[3]

> Your revenue from brokers for finding others for them can be a finder's fee or a percentage of each hour they work.

Well, now the consultant is going to make 60 percent and you are going to make 10.8 percent. You go back to the broker, and after negotiation, they offer $92.50. If you have the perfect consultant for the client, the broker may go back to the client to get more, in which case that may make your increase possible or make it greater. However, the consultant could also be squeezing you at the other end, wanting more of the pie. And each party (broker, you, consultant) wants assurances from the other party that the deal will happen *if* they accept the conditions offered.

> You need to learn to put together deals that work for all parties involved, especially when you want to utilize other people on engagements.

For example, the broker could say to you, "If I can get $10 more per hour for you, do we have a deal?" And you may have to say, "My consultant wanted $15 more, so I need to ask." But before

---

[1]I do not mean this to sound pejorative or as if people who can do broker roles grow on trees. They absolutely don't.

[2]Twenty-five to 30 percent is pretty standard.

[3]Because you are trying to make the deal work, you are taking less than 25 percent.

you ask your consultant, you'd like to *know* that the broker can get the $10 from the client. Otherwise, you're asking your consultant, "If I can get you $10 more, do we have a deal?" to which the consultant may respond, "I have two other offers, and I need to decide today. Let me know if you can offer $10 more." Before the broker asks the client, he says to you, "If I can get $10 more per hour for you, do we have a deal?" and you're back at square one. Nobody wants to move first.

Figure 4.1
When multiple parties are involved in a deal.

The point is that time passes, and it's a long process over which you do not have full control. I'm not saying don't pursue these deals, but prioritize your efforts on them appropriately. The more hands in the deal, the more unlikely that it's going to happen.[4] If you want the utilization of other consultants to be part of your top consultant profile (and most will), as you can see, you will need negotiation skills as much as the skills you will use on assignment (C++, Java, data warehousing, or whatever).

As you grow your abilities as a consultant, you will need brokers less and less. Broker deals are generally *fulltime* and, as just mentioned, they are looking for *you*, not someone else. After the establishment of your practice in Year 1 or Year 2, you should be interested in:

- Higher-rate deals than what most broker deals are offering
- The possibility of placing someone else into the deal
- Part-time engagements that allow you to work multiple deals at once

[4]An exception is when dealing with an H1B consultant, because usually there is plenty of margin in those deals.

- Engaging clients directly
- Not eliminating from consideration those clients who need your services six months to a year from direct service[5]

These mean there will be fewer third parties between you and the client as time goes on. Even after you're more established, you may need to consider using a broker to sustain business and sustain the firm if you are unable to do so otherwise.

In the long term, you will want to get your own deals. Being the sole contractor to broker deals is not the path to the goal I've set forth in the book. You may find, however, that you may be able to work with brokers to split their fees on additional resources you find. As well, you may be able to be a conduit in the sales cycle and gain a fee split—or your next contract, at least—through working with a broker.

You can also find direct clients at these sites. However, many companies use brokers for many of the same reasons companies use consultants—to outsource the work.

Finally, keep in mind that you will likely go under a non-compete with any client you were engaged with through a broker. For 6 to 12 months *after* your *last* day with the client, you will not be able to work for that client except through the broker.

Keep track of your non-competes. Although they may or may not be pursued by the broker, you should sign only those terms you are prepared to follow.

FINDING BROKERS AND CONTRACTS ONLINE

Broker offerings can be found online at all the major job/career sites. Some of the ones with the most contract jobs[6] are www.dice.com, www.linkedin.com/jobs, and www.careerbuilder.com. Don't be discouraged if you see the perfect contract, you apply, and nothing ever comes of it. Most contracts out there are put out in anticipation of landing a deal (and wanting to be ready to go), put out for a low-probability deal (due to lack of client commitment or mass resume submission), or have already been filled. About 85 percent will meet these criteria. Most are also extremely price sensitive. Using online job boards is not a good long-term option.

---

[5]Most brokers will require you to agree to a clause like this. This also puts them in the middle of any add-on or up-sell revenue until the requisite time passes.

[6]See a position you like, but it's offered as a fulltime job? Make an offer to contract for it.

> ### UTILIZING BROKER SERVICES
>
> By utilizing brokers, you may be able to grow your business quite nicely. This is one of the numerous profitable forks in the journey of consulting. You may consider staying a while in broker circles as long as (1) it is your best option for now and (2) you are growing your business.

Business Formation and Taxation

Whether through a broker or direct to the end client, income is income and must be captured in a recognized form for tax reporting purposes. If you're an employee at a consultancy, depending on the structure of that consultancy, you actually may have the same small business accounting issues as mentioned here. Many partners at major consulting firms actually have their own business in the eyes of the IRS.

Most consultants will start their practice as a sole proprietorship. This means you must track your income and expenses and fill out a Schedule C with your tax return annually. If you are not familiar with Schedule C, go to www.irs.gov, download one, and learn about it there. This is really quite an easy business formation for the practice. Its limitations have to do with raising capital and selling the company, which should not be a concern in the first 90 days, as well as in client perception of the small size of the business.

From now on, classify every expense as business or personal. Treat business expenses as if they come from a separate entity... because they do.

Being a sole proprietor also leads many to sloppy recordkeeping. You should do the following to keep a good handle on the business and to keep your time from being dragged into dealing with the IRS (as well as fines, fees, jail time, and other unpleasantries):

- Open a new credit card in the business name and put all business credit card expenses on that card.
- Track cash expenditures for the business and reimburse yourself from the business bank account.[7]
- Write business checks from a business bank account.

---

[7]When clients reimburse your expenses, they are reimbursing you personally. Do not deduct these expenses.

Another very important note is the need to file "quarterly" estimated taxes with Form 1040-ES, as well as any state-required quarterly reports. I put quarterly in quotes because the dates are not exactly every three months. The dates are (currently) April 15, June 15, September 15, and January 15. When you are starting out—and potentially for your career in consulting—it is difficult at best to accurately determine tax liabilities for a year and divide them into four even payments. Therefore, this becomes a quarter-by-quarter decision. Once you have a year under your belt, you can use that as a basis for the minimum quarterly payments required to avoid IRS late fees.

Now is the time to mention adding someone to your team. That person is a small-business accountant. Unless your domain is accounting, you are going to need help with recordkeeping, estimating quarterly taxes, payroll reporting when you start having employees, and staying on top of IRS requirements—current and future. I really do not recommend taking this on yourself unless you have done it professionally. Once you incorporate, your accounting needs will go up as well.

> Consultancies are not unlike any other small business from a formation and taxation standpoint. Small-business ownership education is a necessary part of consulting.

SIDEBAR: FINDING AN ACCOUNTANT

Utilize friends and associates to find your accountant. If the accountant does not have consultant clients but serves doctors, lawyers, and small-business owners, he or she will be able to serve your needs. You must establish trust with your accountant for the relationship to be successful. The accountant's fees, fee structure, and responsiveness are important in the decision process as well. Stay on top of the services your accountant provides so that you can move those services easily should the relationship falter. Given the intertwined nature of your consultancy and your personal finances, it is efficient to have one accountant serve both functions.

Strictly financially speaking, you should wait to incorporate your business until you are at about the $500,000 revenue point. However, you will find that many clients will not deal with you unless your business is incorporated. And you are targeting $500,000 and beyond. I believe incorporation is important to do early for a consulting firm. Incorporation is a simple process, and here are some resources you can utilize.[8]

- www.legalzoom.com
- www.bizfilings.com
- www.nolo.com

Corporation names end in Inc. or Corp. You should use this on all your materials (business cards, website, and so on)—which also indicates that you should get incorporation done before the website, business cards, and so on.

Corporation setup is a multistep process and includes:

When corporation setup is complete, you will receive a corporate tax ID number. You will use this number repeatedly in your practice.

- Determining which state to incorporate in.
- Naming corporate officer(s) (in other words, you).
- Creating bylaws. (Generic bylaws are available.)
- Issuing stock (for example, 10,000 shares at 0.01 per share).
- Setting a fiscal year (such as January to December).

You should file an S-Corporation election for your corporation. This means the corporation itself will pay no taxes, but will pass through its income to the owner's personal return(s). Although there are restrictions to corporations that can file the S election, small consulting firms have no problem meeting the requirements.

THE LIMITED LIABILITY COMPANY

A form of business ownership that has grown in popularity in recent years for small professional firms is the Limited Liability Company, or LLC. Conceptually, it has characteristics of a corporation as well as a partnership. The main thing to understand from a tax perspective is that all income passes through to the owners, just like in an S-Corporation. However, the income can be divided among the partners in any way the partners agree upon, whereas an S-corporation is required to divide income according to ownership percentage. The setup process is virtually the same as that of an S-Corporation.

---

[8]Alternatively, you can ask your accountant for help. The choice is yours.

Partnerships, the third major structure for capturing consulting transactions, are oh-so-tricky to pull off successfully. As its name implies, multiple people will take part in the ownership of such a firm.

Generally speaking, partnerships have more upsides than single-person-led firms. The trick is finding compatible partners with complementary skills, like-minded goals, and agreement on the eventual dissolution process. Partnerships that work run to levels of success much faster than sole proprietorships and single-leader corporations. I have found myself envying those who are aligned as such. Many have certainly outpaced my consultancy. However, perhaps the very reason I struck out on my own is the same reason why I have not found compatible partners (though I have tried)—the need to win, lose, or draw the practice rests with me.

Partnerships are high-risk, high-reward.

Don't get me wrong. I have many times given up control in client situations for a commensurate level of contribution to client success. In a sense, I suppose, I was in a partnership. But it was not a partnership in the legal sense or in the sense of decision making from a corporate standpoint.

Since I consider this usually a downstream activity and consideration in a practice, and because the decisions go up exponentially in a partnership, I cover partnerships in Chapter 15, "Partnerships." Jump ahead and consider a partnership structure if you are working with others in the establishment of the consultancy. Partnerships with vendors, brokers, and so on (in other words, those "partnerships" not involved business formation) will also be covered in Chapter 15.

Insurance

Technically, you may be able to roll for a while without business insurance. However, as with incorporation, prospects may eventually require you to have insurance to do business with them. Specifically, the business insurance required will be general liability insurance. This is insurance that pays for physical and property damage. Once the insurance is obtained, clients will sometimes ask to be a "named insured" on the policy to ensure their protection. This is usually accomplished simply though a fax to the insurance agency. Insurance professionals tell me this does not add any value or extra protection for the client, but it perhaps is a way the client can verify that you have the insurance.

General liability insurance currently runs about $2,250 to $3,500 per year for a small firm. You will have the usual assortment of insurance options to choose from, such as limits per occurrence, firm damage, medical expenses, automobile limits, and excess liability. The "Sample Client Required Insurance" sidebar shows typical client-required insurance needs.

SAMPLE CLIENT REQUIRED INSURANCE

(a) Commercial general liability insurance, with limits not less than $1,000,000 each occurrence combined single limit for bodily injury (including death) and property damage.

(b) Business automobile liability insurance with limits not less than $1,000,000 each occurrence combined single limit for bodily injury and property damage, including owned, non-owned, and hired auto coverage. Commercial general liability and business automobile insurance policies must provide the ability to name various clients as additional insured as required.

(c) Workers' compensation insurance for consultant and consultant's employees.

Incorporation and business insurance—it's a bad strategy to wait until a prospect asks whether you have them, and you say, "I'll get them now."

Be sure to shop around for your needs. The insurance industry, like many, has been thrown into a frenzy with the recession, and prices are currently fluctuating and vary by up to 50 percent from one agent to another.

If your formation is not incorporated, once you begin hiring people to the firm, workers' compensation insurance will be required. This requirement applies to any W2 employee you hire, even if it's for two hours a week. I will cover employee boarding costs in Chapter 10.

Startup Money

I included this section because I am often asked, "How do you finance a new consulting practice?" It doesn't usually cost as much as people seem to think, but read on, because there are some considerations. Keep in mind that if you take the lean-and-mean, client-first, ramp-up approach outlined in this book, you will stay cash-flow positive with the business. A nominal amount, certainly covering the bank minimum to avoid penalty as well as covering the ownership formation, initial marketing, website, education (if any), office furnishings and supplies, and so on, should be seeded into the account. An amount of $10,000 should cover it, which also would be about the amount an employee consultant running their "business within the business" might seek as seed money.

You will be looking to stay cash-flow positive, including after paying yourself a reasonable salary. "Oh," you say, "what's this about salary? I thought I was giving up my salary."[9] The IRS requires that you pay yourself a "reasonable" salary. Once income begins coming into the business, it is well worth checking with your accountant to determine what this minimum salary needs to be. How the remaining income (that is, company profit) left in the business bank account needs to be handled for tax purposes will depend on your form of ownership. This money can be issued to you as dividends, which usually can be taxed lower.

Practically, however, your personal gross profit is your salary, dividends, and retained earnings (the income you leave in the business bank account).

Action Plan

✓ Find, bookmark, and peruse the five best websites for your brand of consulting.

✓ Determine the form of ownership for your firm.

✓ Establish that form of ownership.

✓ Establish a system for collecting business expenses.

✓ Open a credit card in the name of the business.

✓ Open a bank account in the name of the business.

✓ Obtain general liability insurance.

✓ Put the startup money in your bank account.

---

[9]Those who have joined a consultancy most certainly have not "given up their salary."

Chapter 5

How to Stay Current: Technology and Skills

- Focusing Your Technology Coverage
- Mastering Domains
- Technology Environment
- Planning Time for Learning
- Updating Technology
- What If Technology Is Not Enough?
- Action Plan

To make it to the top level of consulting, you will need to become a leader in your area of focus, technically speaking. Clients expect you to be ahead of the curve. You could say vendors define where the market is going. However, top consultants are their accomplices.

Once you arrive as a top consultant, you will stay current as part of doing business. The habits will be so ingrained upon you that you can't help but be current. You will be writing articles and doing speaking engagements. You will be quoted in the press and on the web. You will review product offerings. Recalling the top-consultant profiles from Chapter 1, you may have a significant part of your revenue coming from the vendor community (that is, white papers), where much of the information you need to stay current comes from. In short, you will be a stay-current magnet.

Want to learn something? Commit to giving a presentation on it.

Until that time, in order to be and stay current, I recommend you get involved in all of those activities as soon as possible. I know of nothing better to fully bring your thoughts together than to be forced (externally or internally) to put them into writing or into a presentation.

In my second job (four years out of college), I took a traveling training (a form of consulting) position with a young upstart company.[1] I leveraged my short, but intense experiences into multi-day courses. The company allowed me to swim or drown in front of clients. I supplemented my experience with massive pre-class cramming, and that experience and the knowledge basis it gave me are fundamental reasons why I am a firm believer in speaking (and writing) being great mediums for learning. The experience also taught me not to underestimate myself and how staying 25 percent ahead of my students/clients makes all the difference in the world.

I will speak to the skills and culture of writing and speaking in Chapter 13, "Writing and Speaking," but let me cover some of the other "stay current" items here.

Focusing Your Technology Coverage

First of all, it's a great big world out there, and information is abundant. You could say we are drowning in it. It is not possible

---

[1] Platinum Technology

to be a master of everything. You need to focus your energies. As you consider your desired top consultant profile (as discussed in Chapter 1) and plan your services (which we'll discuss in Chapter 6), you will determine the technologies that you need to master. As well, you will determine the level in which you will need to participate in the knowledge of the technologies.

Primarily, let your experiences with clients and prospects guide you to what you need to know and learn—and learn it well. You will be amazed at how much there is to learn *just* to be a top consultant. A top consultant must survive by his wits and skills and cannot do a half-baked job at mastering a domain. A top consultant will *enjoy* the challenge of displaying his skills. That the skills may have been recently obtained is irrelevant. Most people who *could* learn something deemed optional will never do it. A top consultant will. Those who hire consultants know this.

If you are engaged with a client or a prospect that has a technology in house that is new to you (and which one doesn't?), learn it to at least the "deep conversational" level. You may not be able to go *mano a mano* with the top dog on that technology, but as a top consultant, you are required to put that technology in context of the organizational architecture and the organizational goals, not necessarily deploy deep technological skills.

NOTE

I make assumptions here about the nature of your consultancy. I could be wrong on this point for your individual practice. Another variation to the answer is that your consultants, not you, may actually dive deep into the technology.

As a guru technologist, you will want to learn all you can about the technologies you select. This may be a single product, multiple related or unrelated products, or a single vendor's line of products. In this role, you will also look to people employed by the vendor(s) to direct you in your journey of mastery.

As a higher-level (methodology/architecture/management/analyst-level) consultant, your focus will be less on the details and more on the conceptual knowledge of how various technologies fit into environments. Your technology reach will be broader but not as deep.

Mastering Domains

Regardless of the technologies and the associated depths you select for mastering, there are a few ways to consume the information necessary. They largely involve reading. Reading is something few people in the general population do much of, but it is an absolute essential fundamental requirement for the top consultant. Did your parents teach you to do more than what is required? If not, take it from me—when it comes to learning about your domain, do more than what is required. Read.

Read selectively to stay ahead of the curve.

Today, it is not difficult to learn new technology to the level necessary. Gone is the paradigm that you must dedicate a week, travel, and take an in-person, company-paid course from a live instructor in order to learn anything. If you have that mindset, don't expect to become a top consultant. With the advent of the Internet, there are innumerable websites, posts, white papers, reviews, articles, podcasts, and webcasts available. My favorite method is browsing and reading because it gets the information in more quickly than listening to a speaker *a la* a podcast or webcast. That being said, passive listening may be all that is possible if I am multitasking, and some good information is going to be available in those mediums.

> **NOTE**
> I consider falling asleep one of the activities you can do while listening to a podcast! Ditto for driving.

Only time stands in the way of learning a new skill, given the Internet.

So, what do you read? You should read pretty much everything written in the chosen domain unless and until you find the author, the website, the book, or the outlet to not be useful. You should read critically, knowing that almost every side of an issue will be taken in writing and probably has some validity to it. You are reading not to accept what is written, but to consider it alongside everything in your experience. You are also learning how issues in the field are framed and what people are talking about.

Here are some tips to make sure you are pulling the necessary information into your sphere:

1. Subscribe to all the major magazines in the field. Most are free to people in the industry. I force myself to at least "power flip" through every page in each magazine, and I find just the act of doing that means I stop on the interesting stories and inevitably learn something useful.

2. Sign up for a news aggregator, such as NewsGator or NewzCrawler, and customizable webpages, such as My Yahoo! or iGoogle. You should collect all the blogs useful to you in the aggregator, where the consistent interface lends itself to quick review and searching.

3. Sign up to Twitter (www.twitter.com) and follow those in your field. Over time, more and more people are microblogging, and Twitter is quickly becoming the popular medium for this.

4. Don't forget about books. Toss your keywords into Amazon's browser and see what is selling and what is new in your space. If your space merits a category on Amazon, keep an eye on the bestsellers in that category. Buy the books and learn what is in them even if you don't read them cover to cover.

Do not, however, allow yourself to fall into short-attention-span mode and be distracted by the bombardment of potential reading opportunities. Clients come first. Do all your formal reading and learning during non-billable time. And, please, you can tweet (on Twitter) all you want, but don't get hung up on trying to become the dude with the greatest number of followers.[2]

Technology Environment

As a technology consultant, you must have an environment conducive to interacting with technology. You must be able to install those demo disks and have the curiosity necessary to selectively dive in and learn what some products are bringing to your market.

I recommend that you have at least one modern-specification PC beyond the one used in day-to-day activities. Use this one as a playground for installing and testing technology. Especially if you

---

[2] A Twitterlebrity

are going the technical guru route, you must have an environment where you can actually learn the technologies and their latest releases hands on. You may get lucky and have a client or two provide you with their robust, active business environment in which to do this, but you cannot count on your clients and client billing time to learn technology. You must create that environment above and beyond what clients provide. This is thinking like a consultant and not like a contractor.

Commit to learning.

> **NOTE**
> If your specialty is anywhere near personal computers, you should have more than this minimum.

Planning Time for Learning

Time-wise, it is prudent to pursue your billing and selling activities during the business day and your learning and planning at other times. Marketing activities may take place during either. There are some real-time, business-day components of marketing that may need to take place during the business day.

With this book, you are going to learn all there is to do. If you deviate from the schedule (that is, you are an early bird or a night owl), you still need to make sure everything gets done.

Within the business day, if there is time beyond personal billings, consider the following guidelines for managing the day.

> **NOTE**
> And remember, it's not necessarily your goal to be personally billing fulltime on each engagement; see Chapter 2.

- Make sure you accomplish big objectives daily and not just the little ones.
- Work in organized, clutter-free environments.
- Be conscious of whether email, Twitter, the phone, background music or the television, and so on are actually helping you meet your overall goals. Depending on your personality, you may need to keep distractions to a minimum when doing certain tasks.

- Group like tasks together.
- The bag you carry around should be minimalist when it comes to files.
  - Consciously prune files and papers.
  - Use electronic files where possible.
- The bag should contain everything you need to be productive.
- Utilize calendar reminders (for example, in Microsoft Outlook or Lotus Notes) to remind you not only of meetings, but also of the things you need to do to be effective overall. For example, Wednesday nights might be your "power-flip and read magazines" night.
- Clear the decks at the end of the day and plan for tomorrow.

> **NOTE**
> Somehow I remember each week, without a reminder, to take out the garbage on Wednesdays. Use reminders as needed—the goal is effectiveness, not a perfect system.

Updating Technology

Every year, you should reevaluate the technologies you are mastering to ensure continued relevancy. Have you been able to apply your learning in client situations? Are your clients and prospects asking questions that you can now answer? Have you had enough learning focus so you're a master of a technology? Does the technology continue to look relevant in the marketplace? Is there an abundance of expertise in the market? Have you found it interesting?

Technology can change rapidly, and your employer (if you have one) and clients are not training you—you are.

If the answer to most of these questions is no, consider tweaking your technology set. You cannot change your on-the-job experiences, but you can change your focus for the future.

What If Technology Is Not Enough?

So you're a master of the domain. Now you need to apply that mastery in a client situation, remembering that you are trying to *add value* to their situation. All that knowledge in your head is no good to clients if you cannot apply it. Furthermore—and this is often a tough lesson—most client situations need about 10 percent of your knowledge. However, each one needs a different 10 percent.

To add to your possible shock at this point, get this: Each client situation requires you to work outside your comfort zone. That's the nature of consulting. The tough problems that the client is facing do not fit into a nice, tidy box. If they did, the client would most likely have it solved without you.

Another nuance to all this learning is that while you have to establish your credibility, you don't get to parade your knowledge if you want to be effective. You need the knowledge, but you need to empathize with the client, solve problems, and ultimately add value. If you can do that using more skills than knowledge, then do it that way.

Skills and knowledge are different. Knowledge means you know something. Having skills means you can do something. Both are necessary.

One of the toughest skills to learn is that many clients just need a gentle push, not the forklift you came in with. Unless you are at the pinnacle of personal consulting, doing rent-a-CEO style consulting (and probably not reading this book), you are not asked to come in and change the company. Even if you are, tread lightly with this request.

The forklift approach will not be well received and will only result in backlash. That gentle push and sometimes throttling back, combined with having vast knowledge of your domain, will make you a tremendous consultant.

I have always viewed my engagements as "knowledge sharing." That is, yes, I have skills and knowledge that the client lacks. That's a given, or I wouldn't be there. However, more times than not, somebody somewhere at the client, in my purview, has the solution to the problem. This could be a lower-level employee who upper management views as not being "senior" enough to solve a real problem. It could be someone who does not speak up in the organization. The solution could also be one that needs to be piecemealed together from several opinions in the company. The best solution may be to do nothing. Messing with a "good enough" situation can make it worse, put it on a negative trajectory, and not add the value you desire.

However, the client may not realize they already are doing everything they can be doing. Finally, it may be a solution that just involves two people in the organization communicating—and that won't happen until the smart consultant comes. That's you. Get people talking.

The client absolutely needs you to figure this out for them! The warning here is that the skills that make you a master consultant are not necessarily the technology ones.

Listen to people at the client who don't get listened to. They may have the answer you and the rest of the client are seeking.

Once you determine the solution, communicating and effecting change at the client is yet another challenge. Of course, you have already been somewhat successful with communication if you have secured an engagement, so in the next chapter, we'll plan the services around which we want to win engagements.

Action Plan

✓ Determine the technologies on which you are going to focus.

✓ Subscribe to all major magazines in the field and plan a weekly time to power-browse them.

✓ Sign up to a news aggregator and seed it with relevant blogs.

✓ Follow those on Twitter you can learn from—but don't get carried away in there!

✓ Review your library and check out books you can use.

✓ Ensure that you have the necessary computing power across your personal computers.

Chapter 6

Service Planning

- Categories of Services
- Clients Need Consultants
- Consultants Your Clients Will Want
- Packaged Services
- Training Services
- Project Services
- Action Plan

S ervices are how you're positioning what you intend to do for your clients. It's why they need you. Services are what you've established some unique capabilities around. The services you choose to focus on will depend on your target consulting profile from Chapter 1. If you are Jodi Broker, for example, your services are value-added people. If you are serving the semiconductor industry, you do not necessarily need to know deep, technical details about semiconductors. You need to know some things, and you need to know how to find people in the industry and those who need them in order to be successful with your services.

On the other hand, if you are going to be the Jane Guru of semiconductors and profess guru-level service at guru-level rates, there is a lot you should know about semiconductors—or at least your niche within semiconductors.[1] So, an important factor in setting up your services is what you bring to the table in terms of experience.

I'll cover marketing elsewhere in this book, but keep in mind that ultimately, all deliveries are custom. A "service"—which is a marketing term—will be your best shot at how you want to engage interest on the part of your clients and how you intend to execute.

At www. simplyhired.com, you can check out job trends. Catch a trend on the rise. One of the most difficult things for a consultant to do is let go (cease pursuit) of assignments in jobs with dying interest, where the consultant is not building skills or traction in marketable skills.

The tangible evidence of a service includes its name, an abstract about it, and perhaps some internal documents (intellectual property?) about how you intend to deliver the service. The latter can be shared with a client at the right point to seal the deal.

However, the most important factor is to set services (and fees) to where the market is underserved. Underserved, in this sense, does not necessarily mean there are none of your kind available. There may be none for good reason—the market doesn't need any! Then again, joining the fray when there are numerous consultants already, which obviously verifies a market need, is also not the best approach. Rates will come under pressure as services are viewed as being commoditized. You can always get past the commoditized perception (by doing everything in this book). However, it's still a barrier and must be considered.

---

[1]And since you're still a consultant, you will also need to know how to find people who have a need and possibly fill the need with people they need.

> **STRETCHING TO MEET THE MARKET**
> You should feel free to take calculated stretches to establish a foothold in a service that you believe has some high potential in the marketplace. Say there are no X+Y+Z consultants—or, better yet, there are only a handful of them, but they've stumbled into their success, and you can pass them with a good approach—and you have experience in X+Y, but not Z. Feature X and Y and learn Z. If you believe in yourself and intend to deliver ROI to the client utilizing your services, you will still be delivering a strong value proposition, so stretch yourself.

In summary, the ideal set of services includes those that combine market interest, your experience, and your interest. Barriers to be overcome include too many consultants providing the services and lack of future interest by clients. That being said, as you choose a consulting career, your services should be abundantly obvious based on your expertise.

You must find a way to stand out from the crowd.

Categories of Services

There is a finite set of categories of services that clients are interested in:

1. People, or the proverbial "butts in seats," such as those who will provide the client with expertise in toolsets that they do not have in house.

2. Packaged services[2], such as environment assessments, project plan, and architecture development.

3. Training services, where you give classes, workshops, and other education to the client.

4. Projects where your team completes a bounded deliverable to the client. That deliverable could be a technical implementation, or it could be business results.

The seats that the butts are in are increasingly found offshore—in other countries. Your people could be offshore people.

Ultimately, it's all about what *your* people can do for the client, whether they pay by the hour, pay a fixed rate, or pay in some combination.

---

[2]Note that the "packaged" nature of the services does not necessarily imply a fixed fee. More on fees in Chapter 7, "Establishing Fees."

We'll go through these categories one by one, but keep in mind there is a lot of overlap across the four categories. An engagement may consist of all four categories. It would not be unusual to have a project where you are responsible for the deliverable (Category 4), and you are blending your team with the client's team so realistically you are providing people (Category 1). Said engagement could begin with an assessment (Category 2), which may or may not be treated contractually as separate from the project itself, and finally, the project could conclude with a great deal of knowledge-sharing through client training (Category 3).

The important part to labeling the services is that your language is consistent with the client and that you have open communication about the objectives of the engagement. The other important part to labeling the services is that you will be marketing the services, and you need to convey the value proposition in a few words. You need to create this veil of services in order to engage a prospect, at which point you may customize the offering to suit the needs of the client.

Clients Need Consultants

I could almost make a separate category for "yourself" as something clients want, but it's important to understand all of the information about the requirement to make sure it is a fit for you as well as anyone else. This section is not meant to discriminate between you and anyone else, but it is focused on the requirements for the person(s) by the client.

You fall into the category of people. Your employees are people, and everyone reading this book presumably falls into that category. Six and a half-billion-plus people in the world, but your client wants someone with these characteristics:

E&P data modeling and database design

E&P master data management strategy definition and implementation

E&P data migration strategy definition and implementation

Interface definition for E&P system integration

E&P data storage strategy definition and implementation

Support preparation of business case

Interaction with key stakeholders (business users, architecture group, project manager) in customer's organization as part of the work requirements

Technical Skills Required

Deep understanding of various E&P data types, well header, well logs, production, drilling and completion, seismic, culture data, etc.

Good exposure to various E&P data exchange standards and file formats (WITSML, PRODML, WellLogML, LAS, SEG, UKOOA, etc.)

Hands-on experience of data modeling, data marts, ETL processes and OLAP across in upstream oil & gas, master data management tools and processes, data quality management tools and processes

Good exposure to leading RDBMS, including Oracle, SQL Server, and MySQL

Behavioral Skills Required

Excellent written and oral communication skills

Excellent business presentation skills

Cross-cultural sensitivity

Flexibility to travel as per project requirements

Ability to adapt in ambiguous situations

Desirable Technical/Behavioral Skills

Experience in architecting and/or implementing a data management system in the E&P space

Experience in providing consultancy in the areas of data management (aggregation, business intelligence, data quality, and storage)

Spatial data management and GIS

Exposure to Open Spirit, PPDM, and commercial E&P databases

E&P business intelligence/reporting design and implementation

Behavioral

Ability to adapt to onsite-offshore mode of project execution

Expected experience range: Minimum 10 years and maximum 15 years

Education: Engineering in petroleum or computer science or Masters in geology/geophysics/applied geology

---

From dice.com; Dice ID 10204393; 06/20/2009.

...or at least they say they do. Usually, they will need at least 70 percent of the requirements on their (verbal or written) list. And then they will need 100 percent of something not listed, unless you are adept at asking the right questions in building *your* requirements. Never accept the client's initial requirements as final.

Not only do you need the technical skills requested, but you need to be willing to fit into the rate structure expected by the client. You really need to know quite a bit before you can even ascertain whether this is:

- Possible for you to do
- Possible for someone to do that you have access to, but who isn't you
- Possible for someone to do, but who isn't you or anyone you would have access to
- The client engaged in wishful thinking
- The client being on a fishing expedition and not really having the requisition

Oftentimes, you are talking to people who know what their project requires, but they do not have ultimate authority to bring someone in. Or perhaps they do have authority, but not without gaining more consensus from their superior(s) in the organization. You do not want to accept a person requisition and go to the work of finding a qualified candidate—the process of which is discussed in a moment—only to find out that the client cannot hire the person.

That being said, if I have a qualified resource available, especially an employee who I do not want to lose (and what other kind would you have?), and I come across a requirement that seems to fit, there is no harm in making an inquiry to see whether there is a fit.

Here is the information you need to know about a people resource, including if the client is really asking for you!

- Is the position funded?
- Where are you in your search?
- Can you work with us?[3]

---

[3]This is becoming increasingly important, especially in Fortune 100 companies. You may need to go through a multi-month vetting process to get on an "approved list," or you may need to send your people through an approved source.

- What are *all* skill sets needed, with levels (years of experience) of each skill?
- What are *all* the job duties?
- When can the person start?
- How long is the assignment?
- Is there a target rate range you're looking at?
- Can you pay travel expenses separately, or do you prefer bundled rates?
- What will the process be for choosing the consultant?

Keep asking "Anything else I should know about the position?" until there are no more answers. And then ask it one more time. No, ask it twice. Then ask your value-added questions, because you may know a lot more about what people in the roles do. Unlike what you may think, even after asking 10 people for the person, the client still most likely has been too busy to document the answers to these questions. Also unlike what you may think, most consultants will not want to "bother" the client with difficult questions and will accept the requirements at face value.

If the client will not take a phone call or meeting from you to discuss these questions, that is a very poor sign. Your chance of success is low. Either the client expects you to do all the work of locating the person and *then* they'll react and gradually tell you what you really need to know, or their requisition is halfhearted.

What is at risk here is *your time*. While you must set up an efficient process for securing people you do not employ or know intimately in your warm network, it is still a drain of valuable time to execute that process. It will especially feel like a burden when you present that perfect candidate, only to find out that the client does not have the funds to buy. You will also lose credibility with that consultant.

While you may view the fact that a requirement is posted (for example, on consultant search bulletin boards) as a negative, it is actually at least tangible evidence that the search is not merely a whim. Some small level of investment has been made.

Consultants Your Clients Will Want

Collect people into your network (in the early days) or as employees in your company that fit into the technical profile of the firm's focus (from Chapter 5). Utilize personal contact management, such as ACT!, Maximizer, or GoldMine to store all relevant information.

You should track:

- Names
- Locations
- Skill areas
- Willingness to travel
- Anything you know about their rate requirements
- Full and complete resumes
- Any and all notes you have from your interactions with them, positive and negative

Availability and skill information on consultants has a short half-life, but these contacts often form the basis for your foray into the forest of people.

If you are dealing in only people, unless they are very high quality and specialized people, it is going to be a very challenging environment for you to succeed. Simply put, the Internet has created innumerable places where, with little effort, hiring managers can find talent.

Packaged Services

Much of the consulting advice sticks to selling you by the hour. I want you to think about selling others, too. I also want you to think about selling a more targeted deliverable than your skills deployed for a time period.

Just like people services, packaged services involve selling consultants. Packaged services, however, involve a fixed, or set, deliverable that is specified well before the project begins. It is set by you, not the client. Likewise, the time it is going to take and the number and profile of consultants that it's going to take are relatively set at the outset.

When your sink is clogged, you call a plumber because he has a sink-unclogging service. He may charge you by the hour, or it may be a set fee per sink. Either way, you get your sink unclogged, and all is well. This is a good analogy for selling packaged services because as much as you might sit there and come up with services, they must meet a client need. Sinks get clogged; that's a fact. And we need them unclogged. Quickly. We search for someone who has the service we need.

Think about what your clients need. Clients are busy. While sales cycles can take some time, when a client realizes their need, they look for a particular service. This is a more realistic paradigm[4] than creating services that are designed to suggest to clients what their needs should be. However, you can do some of both. Your breadth and depth of services will depend on what you're looking to accomplish in the market. You might bundle some services together to make a new service.

> **NOTE**
>
> Your strategy could be breadth, which is ability across the full range of services in a domain. This is good for clients who don't quite know what they want, who believe they could very well need more services after the first one, and who would like to know that they won't have to board a new consultancy.
>
> Your strategy could be depth, which is demonstrating some extreme value (such as efficiently getting to the solution, with a tight methodology) in a small set of services. You become the "go to" partner for that service. You may find yourself doing a lot of unpaid self-study to support those services, but it's worth it because of the high-fee and low-sales nature of the services.

Packaged services tend to get a bit gray with building software, value-added services tightly bound to existing software, and reselling vendors' software, which I will talk about in Chapter 15, "Partnerships."

The packaged services that make sense are going to be highly dependent on your chosen domain (for example, Oracle ERP, human resources systems, sales force automation), but some ideas include:

- Environment assessment/audit.

- Architecture development.

- Vendor or tool selection, which may involve a paper evaluation or running a side-by-side comparison or proof-of-concept of the products.

- Writing RFPs for large projects out of your capacity to deliver.

- Roadmaps.

If you have some grist around a service that is requested in an RFP/RFI, you can certainly tout that you can meet the client need spot-on and are not making up the service opportunistically to meet the client need.

---

[4]I knew I couldn't get through this book without using some consultant-speak!

- White papers. (This is geared more to vendors.)
- Webinars and seminars for vendor products or themes they are interested in aligning with.
- Migrations.
- Design reviews.
- Installation services.
- Offsite storage/hosting (more of a subscription-basis pricing method).
- Upgrade services.

Think about how you can collate services your clients are interested in. Those you feel you can estimate, within +/- 10 percent, the time and cost for should become a service instead of just something you or your people do with the time they spend at a client site.

Training Services

You cannot afford to be paid just for the hours spent delivering the training. You must be compensated for the serious effort that goes into training preparation. Although no single client needs to bear the full preparation fee, as a rule of thumb, it takes between six and 10 hours to develop one hour of quality class material.

Training services get very close to the speaking engagements I will talk about in Chapter 13, "Writing and Speaking." There is speaking for free (for the publicity, more seminar-style), and there's speaking for a fee. Training services you offer to your market will generally be longer than the one-hour seminar-style speaking. They will often be more technical in nature and customized. It's really a matter of going back through your market and, as with the packaged services, looking to see what customers might need to become trained in. In effect, training services are a form of packaged services.

Do not underestimate the details involved in training, especially if hands-on labs are involved. Even without the labs, there is the matter of textbooks. Who prints them and binds them? Or are they just electronically distributed? At whose cost? Will a data projector be available, or do you need to bring your own? How many are coming to the training, and do you care (in other words, more students equals greater fee)? Is the room fit for training, or will you be crammed into a makeshift space—or the cafeteria? Will that work?

Clients often underestimate the serious environmental factors that facilitate knowledge transfer in a one-to-many training session. If you are offering training as a service, you, however, should be well acquainted with these factors, communicate them, and ensure they are in place.

Some, especially those with the Jane Guru desired profile, will really need to have seminars/workshops/keynotes in their service offerings. It's a great way to be leveraged and command a high fee.

Well-known celebrities, such as former presidents, Colin Powell, bestselling authors, and so on, command very high speaking fees. These are usually at conferences where hundreds or thousands gather, so that helps spread the fee around. This is not the route to the $500,000 for many people, however—especially in year one or two. These are not workshops either, because nothing much other than their presence and a good speech are expected from the speaker. No interaction. It's good work if you can get it.

> **NOTE**
>
> Training is difficult enough when the students all have cell phones and PDAs. Many operate in normal work mode, with only the occasional glance your way. If you add in the fact that their desks are in the same building, you may have people coming in and out. Talk to your sponsor about what can be done to focus the students and limit outside interruptions. Perhaps a vice president can kick off the training, stressing the importance of being there mentally and physically.
>
> Also, the key to knowledge transfer isn't always what happens in the classroom and the lab—it's what the students do with the information afterwards. You may not be around for that, but you should coach your client on how to reap the maximum post-class benefit from the training.
>
> Oh yeah, and you need to be interesting during the training.

Project Services

Depending on your business model, project services could be what everything else is meant to help achieve. Providing people gives you income without your daily personal involvement in the income, but it's usually on a one-by-one-person basis. Specialized services are, by definition, short in duration, though relatively high-fee. Speaking is high-fee but very short in duration. Project services are multiple people in one shot and long (multi-months or multi-quarters) in duration.

There is also (surprise!) a combining of people and time to accomplish goals for the client. By definition, project services include multiple people. This does not fit the model for Jane Guru. It works perfectly for the John Multicapables.

It may fit David Others or Jane Broker if the client wants them to simply provide the people on the project but not necessarily take overall responsibility for the project. There's a difference, and it's huge. When you own the project, you (your firm) are responsible for its on-time, on-budget completion. You also have leeway in the delivery—people (who/when), project scheduling, and tasks toward completion.

This is where you want to be—if your capabilities merit it.

You may think that, for something as complicated as a multiple-hundred-thousand-dollar, multi-quarter project of strategic significance to the company, the client would always want to give you loads of time to sort through their requirements and work with them to establish a sense of urgency versus risk so you can properly size the effort. However, the reality is that you need to be able to very quickly size up the effort, sometimes on loose cues, and effectively communicate your methodology, including the roles and responsibilities of each team member and significant milestones, if not an outright project plan.[5]

Action Plan

✓ Develop your service list with abstracts and ability to deliver.

✓ Develop your cheat sheet for when you need to take a client request for a person.

✓ Assuming you may want to do projects, develop your methodology for projects in your industry and the roles and responsibilities for the projects.

---

[5]Projects will need project managers, and as the top dog, you may just be that project manager. Check out *90 Days to Success as a Project Manager* by Paul Sanghera (Course Technology PTR, 2009).

Chapter 7

Establishing Fees

It is a necessary exercise to determine what fees you're going to be charging for the services of your firm. There are multiple inputs to fee determination, but broadly speaking, you are looking at the marketplace and the client value of the services.

The more refined the service—that is, the closer you have made it to a "product"—the more justified will be the fee that you desire. If you don't have any of the business items discussed in Chapter 3, you look like a situation that is begging the client for negotiation. If you have a full-fledged offering with lots of material, methodological discussion about what you are going to do for a client and how you are going to do it, and a long list of customers you have done it for, there is not likely to be any negotiation over your suggested fee. The client still may find the fee too high to take on the service, but your fee is justified by the "intellectual capital" that you have invested in the service. You may even want to fixed-fee such a service.

Hourly Consulting Rates

In the previous chapter, we reviewed the various services you could offer. Perhaps the lowest-hanging fruit is per-hour consulting. And since the easiest thing for a consultant to sell is himself by the hour, let's determine what that rate offering should be.

One exercise is to backpedal into what you *want* to make by dividing that amount by estimated billing hours per year to come up with an hourly fee. As interesting and fun as it may be to do this, it is only to give you a sense of what you'll be making in comparison to your salaried friends.[1] It has *no* bearing on what you should charge or what you will receive for your services—none whatsoever.

Let's do the exercise anyway, because it will illuminate some points I want to make.

Such a calculation starts with how many billing hours there are in the year. I use 2,000 hours as a nice round rule of thumb. You

---

[1]Assuming you have your own firm and notwithstanding the extra costs you have that they don't, such as health care and self-employment tax. Adjust the calculation as appropriate, incorporating your bonus structure if you are a salaried consultant.

can multiply whatever rate you are being offered by 2,000 to get a fair comparison. In this calculation, $125 per hour equals $250,000 per year.

In calculating the billing hours per year, there are different starting points. Given the lifestyle integration I suggest between consulting and life, I like to start with total life hours. Except leap years, there are 8,760 hours in a year. Figure a third of those are for sleep, and you have 5,840 as a complete (theoretical) maximum. Okay, so you're getting fussy about weekends. Take them out, and we're down to 4,171 hours. If you only are going to bill eight hours a day, that's 2,085 hours. If you plan to have holidays[2] and two weeks of (planned) vacation per year, you're down to 1,933 hours.

> Yearly is too big a time span for measuring firm success. Use quarterly or monthly metrics to measure success.

NOTE

If you're billing hours, ask to bill more or less than eight hours per day, depending on your ability to work independently, your energy level, and your ability to productively use your time outside of that client. If the assignment needs everybody from the client on site (assuming they work 9 to 5), your focus and energy tend to drop off after eight hours on a job, and you have some productive activities to do for your practice (and you should, after reading this book!), then stick with eight hours. If you have productive hours you can apply before or after everyone at the client has gone home, you have good energy to keep working, and you're not sure yet how to improve your practice after billing hours, then ask to work 10, 12, or 14 hours per day.

Obviously, my 2,000-hour rule-of-thumb does not leave much for non-billing, outside of nights, weekends, holidays, and vacations. But that's the point. Those *are* the times for non-billing activity. Also, assuming I am considering just billing myself, unless I'm working a lot of overtime at a client, I am not counting on much downtime either. That's a profile. You need to design yours.

I logged 3,500 billing hours in one of my first years consulting. I would work one client from 6 a.m. to 2 p.m. and shuttle down the highway to the second client, where I would log 2:30 p.m. to 7 p.m., as well as Saturdays. In addition, I picked up some off-hours

---

[2]Corporations give about nine paid holidays a year.

IF YOU'RE BILLING HOURS, DO YOU BILL ACTUAL HOURS OR EIGHT HOURS A DAY?

Whether it's a long-term or a short-term engagement, you will be faced with a decision about whether to bill for eight hours a day or what you truly work, which is usually more. This is a negotiation item *during* the other negotiation points of the contract, not once the work has commenced. Remember, my rule about asking to work more hours if conditions exist where this makes sense. This is like asking to bill more hours. I contend that if this has not been agreed to beforehand, and you work more than eight hours a day, you still bill eight hours. If you hire contractors, you will need to iron this out with them as well. You don't want them working 10 hours and billing you 10 hours when you can only bill the client for eight hours.

Working hard is a key to consulting success, as it is in any profession. Doctors, lawyers, and big-firm consultants who make the money you want to make are working hard to do it. The shortcut is being efficient, and that's what this book is all about.

fixed-fee white-paper development work.[3] I don't do that anymore, nor do I believe that profile works for most people. However, I've known independent consultants, as well as consultants in large consultancies, who have kept up this pace for more than two decades.

However, despite the emphasis herein on "working smart" to meet the goals we've set, there is undoubtedly a strong, if not more important, element of working hard.

Please keep in mind that unless you are going for the guru profile from Chapter 1, this conversation about how many hours you will personally bill annually is definitely a "first 90 days" conversation. As you get into the second and third quarters, or at least the second year, you should be less concerned with personal billing and more concerned with firm billing.

I, most decidedly, do not want you to get into the trap of bill, seek, bill, seek, bill, seek, and so on. After your first year in practice, you should be looking at leverage and growth. Per the previous chapter, you should have multiple client situations for which you can seek. And, even you guru profiles, unless you're already billing $400 per hour, some time and energy should be spent on continually improving your market offering to raise your rates and package your services.

---

[3] I counted the hours spent on the white papers as billing hours in the calculation of 3,500.

> **NOTE**
>
> Do you bill for travel time—that is, air and train travel to a client site, which is not referred to as commuting? No.[4] Next question. But wait! Don't set up your contracts such that you only bill when you are onsite. You are truly perceived as a beginner and not a true consultant if you have not established a level of positioning with your client such that at least 20 percent of the work can be done offsite. Furthermore, even for you consultants doing very technical work, at least 20 percent of your work efforts should be needed away from the client's systems. Unless you are doing something where little thought is involved, you are productive away from the client's systems, such as on an airplane. Notice I didn't necessarily say away from a keyboard—but you can do that on an airplane. I can't remember the last time I just opened a paperback novel on an airplane.

The answer to how much to charge per hour—and really for all services—is what the market will bear. Know what the market is bearing for your services. You can look at the job boards (discussed in Chapter 4) for a data point, but the best data point is going to be your experience.

Time is your most valuable asset. Long travel to client sites for small amounts of billing doesn't usually make sense. What the

> **NOTE**
>
> Geography has up to a 50 percent bearing on fees. Rates in New York City can be 50 percent higher than in Kansas City, Missouri. However, rates in Helena, Montana may be higher than Kansas City. Why? Lack of local talent and consultant ability to get there easily. I had one client in a small Western town that was isolated from any town you would have heard of by 500 miles. They had to essentially pay New York City rates to lure consultants.

---

[4]Although you can ask for it as a low-importance negotiation point if you're getting hammered on everything else.

client sees is that they are paying (to pick a number) $4,000 for a day, but what they do not necessarily see is the travel overhead to you.

I especially have to be creative to make short-term international consulting make sense. Consider the travel and recovery time over and back (that's two days). Could I do that for one day of consulting? Only if I charge for a few days. And, by the way, I'm more than happy to work the full days for it. Since the requested consulting doesn't take a full day, both sides get creative to find other things—or not.

Rate Flexibility

The broader economy will twist and turn. The economies of your consulting will also twist and turn. They may do so even in the first 90 days. Once you get into real rate discussions with your prospects, their job is to pay less for more. Don't take it personally. Many prospects have hired hundreds of consultants in their career, and they are extremely talented in the art of saving their company money—and, in turn, enhancing their careers. It often looks good just to tell the boss, "The consultant wanted $200, but I got him to take $175."

Before talking about rate flexibility, keep in mind you do *not* want your services to be about rate. The more finely tuned your service and the more confidence you exude (largely from experience) in delivering the service, the less the prospect will question your stated rate.

If the prospect *knows* they will get their deliverable on time and on budget, they may still talk rate, but their position is weakened, and their resolve isn't as strong.

The main reasons why a prospect will want your rate lower are:

- They have always haggled rates down; it's just what they do.
- They are going to have to answer to their management, who will ask them whether they did it.
- They have been burned in the past by consultants who haven't delivered.
- The deliverable you promise is fuzzy.
- They believe it may take longer than you state to get to the deliverable—perhaps they know of skeletons you will encounter.

> **NOTE**
>
> Want to hear someone appropriately state their fee? Call an attorney's office and speak to an attorney about a legal issue you face. When it's time to take the conversation under billing and you ask for the fee, the fee will be stated without equivocation. That's how you state your fee.

So, when do you give in and accept less?

- The prospect is an entry point into a career-enhancing industry.

- The technology to be used is an entry point into a career-enhancing technology.

- The client location is highly desirable, either from a personal standpoint or from a career-enhancing standpoint.

- The application is an entry point into a career-enhancing application.

- You see that the personal service you are providing can lead to multi-consultant services from your firm following this service.

- The work is for a charity or a small firm doing good for society that you want to support.

- Despite your best efforts following the direction of this book, you've been on the bench[5] for a month.

If a client is willing to let you learn on his dime, you should *always* flex your rate for the learning. Future prospects will always weigh actual client experiences higher than self-learning.

If the *opposite* of these factors is true, you would *raise* rates. Keep an eye on the book's companion website at www.90daysconsulting.com, where in the blog I will provide an update at least quarterly on the market conditions for consulting and consulting rates, as well as whether you should think about raising or lowering rates.

Don't worry about the impact of taking a lower rate on what your future rate will be. There's no global database manned by hiring managers tracking rates. Future fees you get will depend on market conditions and your value proposition far more than they will on what your last rate was.

Let's examine the last point—flexing for bench time—a little more. Your ability to adjust to market conditions quickly is an asset of a small firm. Despite the productivity that can be experienced during bench time, it can get quite expensive. This is

---

[5]The bench is that proverbial place where you do not have billing activity going through the firm. There are many productive things to be done during bench time, as outlined in this book. It doesn't have to be hell, but a month without billing should trigger more resolve to get billing, the lifeblood of the practice, going.

Pigs get fat. Hogs get slaughtered. There's a point at which your desire for more is counterproductive.

especially true if you are currently a one-person firm. If you're sitting idle for one month waiting for an opportunity that will earn $10 more per hour, it can take you up to 10 months to break even. Do the math before you decide whether to flex your rate.

Rate Sheet

I despise quoting rates in the first few sentences of an introduction to a client. You should be communicating value. Practically speaking, however, at some point it will need to come up. You don't want to spend too much time selling if the client is thinking $50 and you are thinking $150.

Although you are hoping the client will offer a rate first and hoping your value proposition transcends the whole idea of rate, it is helpful to have a rate sheet available that shows your rate (as part of a category) as well as the rates of all others who you have the capability to bring to bear on an assignment.

Again, this smells of hourly consulting, and that is what we're talking about now. You want to maintain your position as a value-added consulting organization who can eventually fixed-bid projects for clients, so have plenty of that conversation as you pull out the rate sheet.[6]

The rate sheet could look something like Figure 7.1.

> **NOTE**
> Multiply your estimated billing hours by your estimated rate to give yourself a sense of where your individual practice might top out. Think about growth immediately, knowing that an individual practice has limits. Many consultants use figures of $250,000 to $300,000 as the most they can make in an individual practice, although guru-style profiles can make it to $500,000.

---

[6]In 15 years of consulting, I have had to pull out a rate sheet about four times. However, making one forces you to get a sense of what the market is bearing and how different profiles might look rate-wise to a client, both of which are necessary for a thriving consulting practice.

Rate Sheet
Joe's Consulting Company
Confidential
As of 07/01/2009

Senior Principal Consultant $250/hr.
Senior Principal Consultants have at least of 8 years of change management experience and 15 years of project management experience. They are expert large scale integration architects, have tool expertise in multiple tools in project management and process modeling, have broad knowledge of the discipline of business process optimization, are fluent in methodology and have performed numerous referenceable strategic services.

Principal Consultant $200/hr.
Principal Consultants have an average of 5 years of change management experience, 10 years of project management experience, are fluent (certified if applicable) in relevant project management and process modeling tool(s), have training on methodology and have worked on at least 3 referenceable change management projects in positions of high technical responsibility.

Analyst Consultant $150/hr.
Analyst Consultants have an average of 3 years of change management experience, 7 years of project management experience, are skilled in a relevant project management or process modeling tool, have training on methodology and have worked on at least 1 referenceable change management project.

Figure 7.1
Sample rate sheet.

Fixed-Bid Services

If you bring substantial intellectual capital to a client engagement—whether this is in the form of experience or in the form of tools you have developed—that help to jumpstart an engagement and get a client closer to more return on investment (and do it faster than almost any other organization could), you should do one of two things:

- Increase your rate
- Fixed-bid the work

The risk factors to fixed-bid work are aplenty. You have to establish criteria that will trigger the payment. You can suggest the criteria for successful completion based upon what you know you can do. However, the client will want the criteria to be aligned with the objectives that the client has for their business. There will be some discussion on this point.

Furthermore, I know of no project worth anything that can be done in isolation of client environmental factors. You may apply your best efforts to create the "packaged solution in a box" for a client. However, client environmental issues, such as internal support, technical need availability, business unit involvement in communicating specifications and reviewing work product, will vary from client to client. So will your workload. You must do a lot more diligence on the client situation before signing up for fixed-bid work. You will also want to lock down contractually for the possibility of client unreasonableness in doing their part.

> You are not out of the water for meeting deliverables just because you are working hourly instead of fixed. Indeed, many clients will walk you through the fixed-bid process (deliverables, signoffs, and so on) despite the fact that the payment process is hourly.

If you are fixed-bidding work, you are entitled to a premium for your risk. As a rule of thumb, that premium is 30 percent. Estimate the probable time (and expenses, if applicable) to be spent on the engagement (utilizing your rate sheet and covering all resources involved) and increase that amount by 30 percent to cover the unexpected.

One of the most important factors in fixed-bid work is trust. Let's face it: Even after you have done everything you believe you were contracted to do, when client confirmation of deliverables is part of the criteria for payment, at the least, your payment can be held up for a while. At most, if you didn't evaluate the situation appropriately or didn't deliver on time, you are working hours well past your 30-percent buffer, effectively for a low rate and feeling the pressure. It's hard to have trust with new clients, so make sure your capabilities *and* the client situation are lined up well.

> An additional benefit of fixed-bid work is that it escapes the sometimes rigorous bid process that accompanies hourly consulting, which is perceived as commoditized.

Increasing your rate is pretty straightforward. It takes more guts to fixed-bid work. However, if your offering meets the criteria for fixed-bid work, you really should consider it. Once you get over the hump and do one this way, you will be more apt to do them more and more. Your service offering will also pick up steam, and you will be able to do it more rapidly, therefore even more improving your return on time invested.

> With fixed-bid work, to the degree that client involvement is not needed, you should be free to work long hours to accomplish the objective.

NOTE

Some services just beg to be fixed fee. If you have a six-month project and you are billing by the hour, neither you nor the client is going to care much about whether you bill for 1,124 days or 1,124.5 days. However, for smaller (and usually more strategic and higher-fee) engagements, especially those that could take less than a day, these are fixed fee—to protect you.

Billing Variations

There are variations to hourly and fixed-bid work. One of the most common is "not to exceed." This was obviously invented by a client organization. You will have your expected hours to bill, and then there will be another number of hours, perhaps 10 percent higher than the expected hours, that, if you work it, you are allowed to bill it. However, if you work over the "not to exceed" number, you cannot bill for it.

So why would you work those hours for which you are not billing? Unlike an employee, a consultant never needs to work when not billing. This is also a fair question for the aforementioned scenario where you are only billing eight hours a day but perhaps needing to work more to keep up or meet those expectations.

There are various reasons, mostly aligned with the reasons mentioned earlier, as to why you would drop a fee. Always look at the bigger picture of the assignment and your practice when determining whether to work those extra hours.

In Conclusion

In conclusion, when it comes to fees, you need to establish the amount and the form of the fee. Time is your most valuable asset, and your total time invested to receive the fee needs to be considered. Commuting, travel time, and non-billing time count in this regard. If your fee is at any kind of risk, you are entitled to receive a premium for taking on that risk.

While fees are some of the main elements of a contract, there are many others that will be discussed in Chapter 9, "Client Contracts."

Action Plan

✓ Develop your rate sheet.

✓ Design your billing profile.

✓ Apply these principles in setting your fee with your first client.

Chapter 8

The Role of the Consultant

- Consulting Is a Personal Relationship
- Curb Your Enthusiasm
- Credit Is a Four-Letter Word
- Corporations Are Problem Creators
- Consulting Is About Tradeoffs
- Be a Positive Communicator
- Be Very Conscious of Naming Conventions
- The Occam's Razor Principle of Consulting
- What Could Go Wrong?
- The Use of Guiding Principles
- Action Plan

Prospects are prospects until you get a signature on a statement of work stating that they are going to pay your company for services you provide. Then, they become clients. However, they are also prospects while they are clients. They are prospects for the next service—the one after you complete what you are currently contracted for. This is the so-called *follow-on* work.

If you cannot secure follow-on work, you will not be successful as a consultant. Follow-on work is simply payback for all the effort it takes to put yourself on the client radar, for them to become a prospect and finally a client. This is not simply about the energy put into those companies who become clients. It's about the time, energy, emotions, and money you put into developing the marketplace. In other words, you need those few companies who actually become clients to pay for all of the touches you make to those who don't.

Clients are the best prospects.

Life is short. Those who do come into our circle in this journey should be treated as special. Call it fate or whatever, but by some stroke of coincidence, James Joseph and Franz Sanchez became your clients, vendor contacts, other consultants you associate with, or high-value prospects who you've spent some time with. Don't lose that by becoming complacent in the relationship.

The lines also blur in time spent working as a consultant. I honestly don't know how to answer the question, "How much do you work?" Well, it depends—does that include reading, learning, attending webinars, traveling (am I working at client dinners?), and so on? If you enjoy what you do, it does not matter how much time is spent working.

This is not about a "put on" relationship where you really don't like the person and are faking enjoying the person in order to see what they can do for you sometime. If someone truly rubs you the wrong way, you have my permission to blacklist that person. However, you should always check yourself when you do this, because getting along with others is a key correlate to success. You already have something in common with people you come in contact with in your business. Furthermore, most people have something to give you in a relationship, and it really should be a matter of what degree your relationship will take on, not whether there will be a relationship.

You may be great in this area, or you may need to work at it. True value-added consulting is business, but it's also personal. Some will struggle with this new way of relating to people. It can be a difficult transition for those who have always been employed by others and have maintained a mental distinction between business and personal. With consulting, the lines blur.

It is the relationship, as well as the delivery, that turns the prospect into a client and the client into a repeat client. This chapter deals with the sometimes complicated, exhilarating, seldom linear, and often frustrating process of the relationship between consultant and client.[1]

Consulting Is a Personal Relationship

In Chapter 1, I talked about abstracting the personal relationship into a set of numbers, or deliverables, in the form of return on investment for the client. I need to caveat that now. Your success with your clients will be measured by your measurable impact, but if you deliver that in a dour or confrontational manner, that impact will certainly be discounted, if not outright voided.

Consulting is a personal relationship. You do not want to compound the fact (and it is a fact) that a client's problems are usually people problems and not technical ones. The consulting you aspire to means you must deal with the people issues behind the complex problems at a client.

Though brought in under the guise of implementing a technical solution to solve a problem, I have seldom seen real problems be caused by technology. Technical implementations, if they go well, will undoubtedly gloss over corporate problems for a while, but the corporate problems will return. Attending to the post-implementation client roles and responsibilities for success is part of true consulting.

The following sections contain some tips for dealing with people and engagement issues.

Curb Your Enthusiasm

If your estimations of value that the client is going to receive seem otherworldly, present a reduced, yet still acceptable, measure of success. I remember formulating one projected return on investment that was in the 500-percent ROI stratosphere. Obviously, the client is going to want to do this, right?! Imagine getting a 500-percent ROI. Fortunately, this consultant was counseled by his client to chop it down to 10 percent of the estimate—50 percent ROI. That's still an eye-popper, but at least it's a more reasonable estimate in the eyes of the executives who would be approving the project. The project was approved and had a good

Your projections need to be kept reasonable.

---

[1]And prospect, although I will refer to both client and prospect as "client" for simplicity's sake.

outcome—but more in the 50-percent range than 500 percent after all!

The point is that there certainly is a "good enough" threshold for project justification. Stop with the projected benefits when you get there. Don't look ridiculous by promising to single-handedly solve all their problems—and end world hunger while you're at it.

If what you are proposing does not show acceptable project benefits, then it's not worth doing. Don't propose it. However, all companies need help and have ROI-producing needs right there under your nose. Don't be a one-trick pony. Be creative enough to keep working on your project justification until you show meeting a real need with a real project.

Credit Is a Four-Letter Word

The topic of project justification brings with it the whole matter of credit. Credit in consulting is a four-letter word. If you are looking for pats on the back, consulting may be the wrong field for you. Here's what you want out of a consulting engagement:

- To be paid according to the contract.
- To obtain a reference and/or a referral.
- To learn something of significance.
- To secure a client[2] for life.

Don't look to receive credit; look to give and cause credit for others.

If you only achieve the first goal, you are not allowed to be unhappy. However, you certainly should do whatever is in your control to accomplish the second, third, and fourth goals as well. At a lower scale than a reference is pure appreciation. You should ask for honest feedback on your or your team's performance at various intervals during the engagement. However, it is not usually a client priority to provide the feedback—unless, of course, you are failing miserably and their career is affected.

You are the one who ultimately needs to know whether you are providing good work and good value to the client. Do not be hung up on making sure the spotlight is on you and your work. This kind of hang-up is an albatross to success for a consultant. There sometimes is a complex chain between the client admitting there was a

---

[2]People move around, so securing a client for life can refer to either the client company or the client person...or both.

problem and wanting to do something about it. This doesn't always translate into you being the solution. In fact, the best mindset to have about consulting is that you are there to *help the client succeed*.

Corporations Are Problem Creators

Speaking of problems and solutions, ever since man first decided to work together to bring down the beast, disagreements about the collaborations between people have existed. The process has been refined over the years, and there is a normative business behavior pattern. However, this has not erased conflict. The rapid consolidation among corporations these days actually exacerbates human interaction issues. And, folks, humans create the problems that other humans fix.

I get involved in client problems so deeply that sometimes the only seemingly sane thing to think is that once the problem is solved, as complex as it is, it's smooth sailing from there for the client. Wall Street will love it, the stock will jump, sales will rise, competitive advantages will be locked up, and the competition will be doomed. I love solving problems, but there's always another one. It's like a balloon where once you squeeze one end, out pops a bubble at the other end. Squeeze it, and…well, you get the picture. Problem number two—a distant, uninteresting problem two weeks ago—is now priority one.

Keep an eye out for your client's problems that you can solve…er, help them solve.

Client solutions are often known by the client—just somewhere else in the organization and not the person you are talking to. Be that person who seeks out those opinions and, if they have merit, surfaces them (with due credit if the originating person wants it). Especially at lower levels, employees are often stifled in expressing their opinions, but this does not mean they do not have valid opinions.

Be on the lookout for ways you can help your client beyond what you were brought in for. There are always problems to be solved.

Consulting Is About Tradeoffs

It is a tremendously key skill to be able to articulate various ways to get to an end state. These end states usually come with tradeoffs that look like this:

Aggressive	*Risk Adverse*
Lots of people on the project	Fewer people on the project
Large goals	Small goals
Aggressive timelines	Manageable timelines
High risk	Low risk
Low business involvement	High business involvement
Just the end goal	Interim goals along the way to an end goal

Your client may be pushing you into one extreme or the other, only to find out he is ultimately not willing to live with the tradeoffs that come with that selection. For example, you are asked to complete a project in three months. You think that is very reasonable, so you only bring one additional person with you to accomplish the task.

One month into the project, something seems to have changed. The client is suddenly looking at the project for the deliverables. Perhaps he shares with you some of the new pressures that he is under; perhaps not. Either way, it's time to get more aggressive with the project. You may need to move toward the aggressive side of the tradeoffs. While you should have had the tradeoff conversation with the client already, it's now time to lay out some new possibilities for the client. You can add another person and meet the deliverable goals more quickly. You can cut some corners to get to the deliverables more quickly. You can more sharply define the expected deliverables so you are *sure* you are working spot-on to the specific, grievous problem. You can enlist more support or involvement from the client team. Et cetera... You need to know your deliverables well enough to present these alternatives *at all times*. You furthermore should be sensing the "tea leaves" of the project and *suggesting* the alternatives that make sense for the client.

> Too many consultants only present alternatives to the client that make sense for the consultant—and they look greedy in the process. Good consulting always takes client needs into consideration first in communicating tradeoffs.

> I have never said "I can't" to a client. There is a way. It may be a tradeoff to be considered, or it may be a tradeoff to be determined. Deem yourself capable of investigating alternatives, perhaps even suggesting another consultancy to handle an aspect of a client problem if they will provide better ROI to the client than your firm will.

Most environments resemble a mishmash (yes, that's the technical term) of the good and the bad. It's a combination of well-architected structures and those that were obviously designed to meet an urgent need regardless of the longer-term consequences. This dualistic reality is true for all organizations.

Are the well-architected structures right and the others wrong? That depends on your perspective. There is no easy answer. However, there are effectiveness and efficiency measures. Effectiveness is measured by the client's ability to meet specific needs—and how long they are going to be able to do so with current support levels before re-architecting is necessary. A quick and dirty solution may meet a singular short-term need in a timely and very effective manner, and it may be well architected when you don't consider the longer-term needs. However, it is efficiency that usually enforces good solution architecture.

For example, many corporate programs still operate using fairly rudimentary, home-built solutions that conform to no guidelines. As the needs grow—and especially the need to integrate—the patchwork approach required to pull together the disparate structures grows too...and it becomes painful.

Essentially, these departments wish they had a more suitable corporate approach, where all the requirements—both now and in the future—can be met, so that they can immediately exploit the data or quickly add it when needed. How long until they bite the bullet and consolidate into a "bigger hat" solution? It will likely happen, but when? However, if the unarchitected components meet the need accurately and in a timely fashion, it is difficult to argue that the solution is wrong.

Be a Positive Communicator

Playing the blame game happens all around us at all times. Sometimes it's subtle; other times it's quite overt. What seems to happen once an employee leaves? Often, his or her peers suddenly find out that he hasn't been doing a good job after all, and the company is better off without the former employee. This is a form of the blame game. The reality usually is a form of the fact that everybody does things different and has different opinions.

Coders use different coding standards. Project leaders take different approaches. Sometimes methodologies don't translate to different technologies. And timing is everything—we don't know the tradeoffs that were in effect in situations in the past, especially under different management regimes.

When you enter a client situation, to make yourself look better, you may be tempted to cast all manner of dispersion on the situation you find—and, by extension, the people (some gone and some still there) who helped to create the situation. The client may even be expecting you to do so. As a consultant, you have to identify the problems as you see them, and the client is owed your opinion. However, be judicious with blame. Your focus should be on the future and how to get there.

If you suggest any kind of change, some will get their feathers ruffled. It is inevitable. Once I did an assessment of a client environment. It turned out to be an evaluation of a project that had been done by another consultancy. Interestingly, the executives who received my report decided to share it with everyone currently on the team. That's their prerogative, and unless I know ahead of time that there will be a very limited readership of my

You need good sense to minimize alienation and keep the client focused on a better future. It is never my intention, as a consultant, to see client personnel replaced. That is a client decision. I objectively point out the pros/cons and best way forward with the situations I find at the client.

deliverables, I don't write anything I wouldn't want anybody in the company reading, should the sponsor of the work choose to share it.

Each recipient was invited to formally reply to the report anonymously. Here's the point: Despite my objectiveness, the responses ranged. At one end of the spectrum, people thought I was treating the consultancy with kid gloves because, after all, we consultants "protect each other." At the other end of the spectrum, some people thought I was overly critical of the project. Everybody has their opinions.

Be Very Conscious of Naming Conventions

Industries that spawn consulting organizations to support them have a very difficult time reining in the nomenclature of that industry. With every vendor and consultant trying to leave their mark on the industry, acronyms are created left and right, and once-sacred definitions are continually nuanced, if not outright replaced. Eventually the phrasings become meaningless. It all depends on who you talk to.

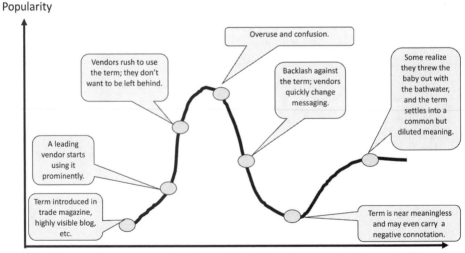

Figure 8.1 *The lifecycle of a term in a thriving industry.*

The point is that you can look for your opportunity to inject your definition into the industry if you wish to join that fray. An effective alternative—and one that your clients might appreciate—is to speak (and write) to clients as if they are being bombarded by overlapping definitions in the industry you represent, full of hard-to-follow homonyms and synonyms (because they are). Example consultative talk might include, "You may hear OLAP referred to as any kind of data access, or you may hear it referred to as specific forms of data access that include the ability to see your business metrics by any business dimension."

Labels are not used consistently.

If the client happens to want to go with some definitions that seem to be working in their environment, go with it. You should be flexible enough to accommodate them. However, the efficiency and convenience of everyone being on the same page with their references is unmistakable. If there is opportunity, you can then feel free to forge your chosen definitions into the client situation. But do so with the caveat that they may hear or read different definitions of the term and/or different terms used to describe whatever it is you're describing. And do so with the explanation of why labeling is important.

When it comes to naming conventions and labeling, the consultant must also guard against his or her own prejudices, or it will soon become evident that the consultant and client are clearly on different pages. Confusion does not a good relationship make. When you see a problem at a client that you've seen before, sure, it's great that you have the experience fixing it. Just remain vigilant throughout the process in case flexibility is required.

The Occam's Razor Principle of Consulting

Occam's Razor (paraphrased) states that the simplest explanation is usually the best one. At some level, there is a finite set of problems that clients may be having that you are addressing. Think about your client (past and future) situations that you may be called on to address. On one page, list them out. At a high level, something should be done about each situation that you want to influence in the client relationship.

For example, you may find software that is so old that its vendor refuses to support the client anymore. Not only is this causing all manner of support costs and delays, but the client is likely missing interesting new features that the client is building workarounds for. Quite often, these client cultures lack an understanding of the importance of staying relatively current with their chosen technology. Instead of perpetuating complex workarounds, it may be the upgrade is the simple lever to turn to produce the best results for the client.

The simple answer to a client problem is often the best one.

You are looking for leverage at a client. You are looking to make a small change that will result in the biggest impact for the client. It is only reasonable to assume that, in most cases, despite your best efforts, you are only going to be able to make one small change at a time. Make immediate impacts by effecting small changes with as large of results as possible. If the results are not large but at least progressive, look to make continued immediate impacts that add up. Coming into an organization—especially a large one—looking to make big changes without the intermediate steps is tantamount to failure.

What Could Go Wrong?

Once scope is set for an engagement, the best question for a consultant to ask (themselves and others) is, "What could go wrong?" Once you know the answers to this question—and keep asking this question until there are no more answers—you can then set about taking care of all of those factors and increasing the chances of success with the client engagement. By the way, even if you think you know all the answers, ask people at the client for their answers to the question. They will tell you.

Recalling that consulting is about tradeoffs, if you do not have the resources to reasonably take care of all possible negative outcomes, these belong in your communications with the client.

This is also a way of tapping into your inner thoughts and bringing them out into practice. Consulting is a mental game, and one difference you must bring is the ability to see what others don't. The best way to draw that out is to continually ask questions, and the best one is, "What could go wrong?"

The Use of Guiding Principles

Finally, every organization should work from a methodological approach. However, the approach needs to be tempered with accommodation for urgent needs. A plan for getting back to the desired methodology and architecture should accompany these approach details. Let's call it all *guiding principles*.

Guiding principles include the exception conditions for their use. However, what if an urgent need arises for data in a "quick and dirty" manner, and your latency factor for building the solution in an elegant structure is too slow to meet the need? You can correct this systemically—as you probably should—but there's no one to step up with the budget for this now. The proponents of the urgent need can argue that is not their burden to bear, and they would be right.

Yet don't give up on your guiding principles too easily. They are worth fighting for. Usually, after adding a few basic processes to the environment, architected solutions are quicker to come by than unarchitected ones.

This is the essence of a hybrid, best-of-breed approach. It accommodates the urgent needs of the business while adhering to a flexible, scalable approach that will ultimately provide the most effective balance of both efficiency and effectiveness.

I'm sure most of you can appreciate these mixed messages that are commonplace when advising on areas of judgment. Consulting is a judgment issue—both initially and on an ongoing basis.

The chances of successful efforts significantly correlate to having people with the right characteristics for success on the project—or at least enough of them to compensate for those who do not have the right characteristics. Also, success goes far beyond technical skills, and good technical skills need to be balanced with communication and direction-setting.

An overriding characteristic needed is sound judgment or the ability to arrive at and act on a consensus of opinion, including:

- The ability to arrive at a rational consensus within a group
- Respect for and understanding of the validity of other viewpoints
- Putting the good of the group ahead of the individual

Putting together the what, when, and who has created the most successful consultant-client relationships in the world.

Action Plan

✓ Make a list today of whom you can help get credit from their superiors at work.

✓ Identify the buzzwords you use and identify how the industry and your clients may be using the terms.

✓ List the problems you will typically find at clients and their most simplistic solutions.

✓ Develop approaches to uniquely provide those solutions.

✓ Decide to be a positive communicator.

✓ Ask yourself "What could go wrong?"…and take care of the answers!

Chapter 9

Client Contracts

- Master Services Agreements
- Administrivia
- Statement of Work
- Action Plan

Usually, the client signature on a contract is one of the last tangible steps the consultant can use to indicate they, or their firm, are on the way to being paid. However, contracts do not just arrive at your doorstep for signature, and there is a significant process that precedes the written representation of an agreement. The most significant components of the agreement should have been agreed to verbally, making the contract a formality. However, establishing the written contract is seldom the formality that it should be. The contract time is when the assumed but unspoken comes out. It's also when the tedious details that neither party had the energy to focus on during talks come out.

Technically, a contract does not *have* to be in writing. Realistically, contracts *should* be in writing.

A contract is an agreement between two parties to carry out mutually legal actions. The parties must be competent upon entry to the contract. Also, the contract must specify the actions that each party is taking as a party to the agreement. We could agree that we like each other, but without either of us doing anything—such as me doing some work for you and you paying me—it is not a contract. Contracts are an essential part of the process of engagement. If you are running the consulting company—or your company within a company that is a practice—you must become familiar with the contracts process and the terms that you will routinely encounter.

Acting like a big shot who's in a bidding war that you're not really in is high risk and is not recommended.

It's a judgment call, but generally I advise against believing a deal is done and foregoing active pursuit of other business that would limit your ability to do the deal until a contract is signed. It's "all systems go" pursuing other business until the contract is signed. Then, you have a commitment to the client, and if something better comes along—assuming you can't do both—you should keep to your commitment at that point. You need to avoid disappointing the prospects in this process, which is why you generally need to advise each prospect of your urgency factor.[1]

While you are welcome to mentally prepare for a project and make tentative plans, it's those costly and unrecoverable expenses and opportunity costs that you cannot incur without a contract. These include beginning work, booking travel, and contracting any outside resources or otherwise seriously blocking out your time and your team's time for work without a contract. You will almost never—but never say never!—want to suggest beginning

---

[1] They don't always have the same consideration for you, but try to be a bigger person than that.

without a contract (and most clients would not take you up on that anyway), but occasionally clients will ask you to do this, and you may if the upside is great and you are relatively hungry for business.

What many new consultants do not realize is that, in many cases—especially in large companies—you will deal with someone who ultimately only has the power to suggest or recommend that the mutual agreement be done by the client. Someone higher up, a central contracts group, or both will ultimately determine whether the contract will be executed.

To say you refuse to deal with anyone but a final decision maker would cut you off from way too much opportunity—if you expect to deal with midsize and larger organizations. However, be *sure* you understand the level of authority of the person you are dealing with. They may need to be prompted to begin to get whatever other buy-in will ultimately be needed. Do not expect them to be necessarily concerned with *your* need for a contract. Mostly, they have not been consultants themselves, and many will not understand your need to trigger movement around the contract at an appropriate early point in the relationship.

Leading up to the contract, a significant process will occur that includes a determination of scope, rate and terms of payment, travel expense handling (if applicable), and location of the work. Most likely, it will also include who will be doing some or all of the work. A client will want to see this part of the agreement, as well as your various and sundry terms, in a written contract that you will need to create.

There is this basic contract or statement of work (SOW) that you will create for the client. There also may be a client-side "blanket" contract containing their standard terms for all contracts. This can be called a *master services agreement* (MSA), a *services agreement*, or something else. Whatever it's called, it's a contract. If you even entertain the idea of doing a contract with them, many clients will present you with an MSA. Some will ask you for yours. Be prepared to present it. The MSA is often a required prerequisite to a contract for actual work. I prefer to avoid the MSA and put all terms in the SOW, but clients may want both, so be prepared.

In anticipation, you should work with your attorney to draft your preferred MSA as well as a generic SOW or two. If the client has an MSA process, you will generally need to work from that as a

I have done *gratis* consulting when necessary to prove myself and gain a large contract. However, I do so with a contract that specifies $0 initial rate and strong-enough language that tries to certify a real rate if metrics are met in the initial period.

Client control is a term you may hear in consulting. This is desirable. Many use it to refer to getting clients to do what you want them to do. I prefer to use it to refer to the fact that I do not have control over someone else, but I do assert my needs into the process and eliminate surprises. This is desirable client control.

Whatever you sign—an MSA or a contract—be prepared to live with all the terms.

basis. Negotiate any points you are not comfortable with. You may want to send all MSAs and SOWs that do not come from your attorney to your attorney before signing. I say this fully acknowledging the expense and potential delay associated with it.

Master Services Agreements

The MSA is a contract that is essentially a terms agreement. It contains terms that will apply for a defined period of time between the two parties. Its covenants will be applied to all SOWs entered into by the two parties unless a countering term is used in the SOW itself. The idea, however, is that the agreed terms will persist through all the SOWs in the period. Therefore, the agreed terms have legs, and each should be carefully considered. Those consultants who have joined firms will find that the firm already has an MSA it likes to use.

Without an MSA, you may still do business with MSA-required companies, but you will have to subcontract through a firm that has an MSA with the company, losing revenue in the process.

Getting into an MSA with a client is often a very important step and can indicate significant future business with the client, as many clients have a limit to the number of MSAs they give out.

In the following sections, I'll address some common terms found in MSAs. Keep in mind that these terms may very well end up in the actual SOW. It depends on how both parties wish to structure the arrangement. The distribution of terms between an MSA and an SOW is usually directed by the client, although with smaller clients, they could easily take your direction.

Opening

To give you a feel for how an MSA might characterize itself, here is a typical opening paragraph for an MSA:

> This Master Services Agreement (the "Agreement"), effective as of April 18, year (the "Effective Date"), is made by and between Circuit Associates, Inc., a New York corporation ("Circuit"), with its principal place of business at 123 Main Street, New York, NY 20013, and Big Client USA, Co., a California corporation, with its principal place of business at 456 Elm Street, Chicago, IL 38535 (each a "Party" and collectively, the "Parties"). Pursuant to this Agreement, Circuit will perform services for Big Client and its Affiliates (collectively, the "Big Client Entities", and each a "Big Client Entity") under the terms and conditions stated herein.

Then, there are various recitals and definitions. There is seldom an issue with this section, because it is the context of the terms that is important, and that comes later.

However, either in definitions or otherwise, it is not unusual for the client to want you to acknowledge your professionalism—something like, "Circuit agrees that consultants will perform the services with at least the standard of care and quality usual in the business process reengineering industry." Clauses like this may seem meaningless, and indeed the client has responsibilities in the relationship to identify and curtail unprofessional conduct; however, many engagements are allowed to run (sometimes well into the millions of dollars) without much client oversight. If deliverables don't happen, everything is on the table, including your professionalism. Make sure that not only are you in high communication with the client about progress (see Chapter 12), but that you are delivering, and there should be no problem. Although various things may be questioned in the relationship, no serious question of your professionalism should occur with your work if you follow the direction herein.

Delivery results are not correlated to consulting company size. Smaller firms deliver just as much as larger ones, although some measure of prestige remains for the larger ones. This is eroding, and as this realization sinks in, the market is moving toward firms that deliver for them, regardless of size.

Personnel

The MSA is not where you would get into specific individuals on assignment. However, there might be some overriding clauses that the client may wish to apply to the people-engineering of their projects. Ideally, you fully control the personnel placed at the client. Clients may think otherwise and choose to retain the ability to:

- Interview all prospective consultants on their project
- Request replacement of any of your consultants on their project (usually with a notice period)
- Insist that only your W2 employees are used on the project

For example, the following represents one such clause that may be found:

> If at any time, Big Client is dissatisfied with an individual consultant's performance, Big Client shall promptly report its dissatisfaction to Circuit, and Circuit shall immediately take steps to remedy the dissatisfaction. If after two weeks a mutually agreeable solution cannot be found, the concerned consultant's work shall cease, and Big Client shall not be liable for

the Service fees in regard to consultant from the time of such termination. Big Client's sole liability in such event shall be to pay Circuit, in accordance with the applicable Statement of Work, for the Services actually performed by such individual(s) prior to the termination.

These are business issues, not legal ones. If the client is dissatisfied with the performance of a consultant, the client may very well be dissatisfied with the entire operation and exercise their right to terminate the contract, which can usually be done on a two-week notice. Pick your team carefully to begin with and set them up for success. Monitor progress and ensure client satisfaction. If it comes to consultant replacement, you must be nimble enough to do it (see Chapter 10, "Acquiring People") as either self-directed[2] or client-directed. If you're not, then don't take on a multi-person project.

> Make sure any termination rights by the client—individuals or the entire project—can be executed only with at least two weeks' notice.

Confidentiality

Clients will want to limit what you say about their business to others. This is, hopefully, understandable. They don't want their business strategies—what's working and what's not, what markets they're moving into and out of, what products are under development, what executives are coming and going, and so on—to be known by their competitors. So, they restrict you from telling anyone so that anyone does not tell someone else, who tells someone else, who tells the competitor.

A sample and acceptable clause may look like this:

> For purposes of this Agreement, "Confidential Information" of a Party to this Agreement means information or materials disclosed or otherwise provided by such Party ("Disclosing Party") to the other Party ("Receiving Party"), including, but not limited to: (a) information relating to the business of the Disclosing Party, including marketing, products, identity of suppliers, partners or franchisees and product or supply pricing information; (b) any unannounced product(s) or service(s) of the Disclosing Party; (c) the terms, conditions and subject matter of the Contract Documents; (d) all information and

> Confidential material does not have to be labeled "confidential" unless the contract specifies that. If you find the definition of confidential material too broad, you may want to define it more specifically. Some definitions presented actually inhibit the ability to do the work that is being requested. Note that if the information becomes public (and not by you), you can talk about it.

---

[2]When you do it as self-directed, some clients will opportunistically ask why you didn't do it earlier and begin to over-critique that person's work product. Be prepared to defend your timing.

reports that may be generated by the Disclosing Party pursuant to any Statement of Work; (e) interim reports and Work Product that may be generated by the Disclosing Party in connection with the Contract Documents; (f) all Work Product; (g) proprietary methodologies, techniques and tools of the Disclosing Party; and (h) any other information or Materials that are designated as "Confidential". "Confidential Information" does not include information that: (i) was known to the Receiving Party, without restriction and without duty of confidentiality, at the time of disclosure, as evidenced by the written records of Receiving Party; (ii) is or becomes part of public knowledge other than as a result of any action or inaction of the Receiving Party; (iii) is obtained by the Receiving Party from an unrelated third party without a duty of confidentiality; (iv) is independently developed by the Receiving Party without reliance upon or use of the Confidential Information of the Disclosing Party; or (v) legally required to be disclosed by the Receiving Party under a requirement of a governmental agency or court of law having jurisdiction, but only if: (A) the Receiving Party provides the Disclosing Party with prompt notice prior to disclosure so that the Disclosing Party may seek judicial protection; and (B) the Receiving Party discloses only that information which, in the reasonable opinion of its counsel, is required to be disclosed. Big Client shall be free to use and/or disclose all Work Product as it shall determine in its sole discretion.

This extends to the safeguarding of all materials that the client may provide you with that pertain to their business that they do not want made public. You will also sign that you will return such information at the end of the contract. Use common sense in protecting client information in any form and when talking about your client work with others.

Some clients will also want to limit your ability to even publicly disclose the fact that you are doing work for them. There could be several reasons for this, but it mainly centers on controlling the public image of the company. They are unsure what language you may want to put around your message. Public companies especially may be sensitive to the public knowing about the projects they are doing. If they are doing business process reengineering, for example, somebody may think (1) they have business process problems and (2) these projects don't work, so they're still going to have the problems after you're done. When dealing with the public and all the perceptions—right and wrong—that people will have, ordinary rules are thrown out the window. This is why those companies have public relations departments and why your messaging will often have to go through them.

Get the client to contribute quotes to your press release. A press release for an engagement win is nice, but one for engagement success has much more impact.

References are vital to your reputation and your ability to get future business. In my opinion, the inability to publicly display a client logo (as your "client") is a grave concession. Try to reword these clauses to indicate that you can use the client name/logo and can do a press release on your successful work, with the press release being mutually agreed to before release. This obligates the client to work with you to craft something they can live with.

Payment Terms

In an MSA, payment methods are discussed. Specific rates are not. Most MSAs have clauses for "if the SOW is fixed" and clauses for "if the SOW is T&M." Even if you do not think you will do one or the other of these methods with the client, review each clause for alignment with your expectations.

Fixed-fee work requires three to five times the paperwork, but it is worth it.

Innumerable terms may be added by the client around payment. (Recall the fee discussion in Chapter 7.) However, of all the sections in an MSA, this is the one that is most overridden when it comes to the SOWs. The thing to be careful of is agreeing to blanket terms in the MSA and *not* overriding them in the SOW. For example, an MSA may say that a fixed-fee SOW, despite what deliverables may be listed in the SOW, is considered delivered only under the sole opinion of the client. In other words, no objective criteria. This leaves you exposed. You can choose to fight it here or in the SOW, but don't forget it.

Payment terms discussed here also have to do with the duration of the "net" period between invoice presentation and payment, how frequently you can invoice, and what, if any, penalties there are for late payments.

Rights Ownership

In normal fee-for-service arrangements, the client will want to be sure they will be able to use the work product for its intended purpose—to improve their business. And unless you're selling software, they will not want to be bound to paying maintenance fees to you.

The following clause is an example:

> All Services rendered by Circuit, and its affiliates and subcon-
> tractors and their respective employees, officers, directors and
> shareholders, and the product or proceeds of such Services,
> including, but not limited to: (a) all written documents,
> schematics, designs, code, disks, tapes, drawings, reports, spec-
> ifications, papers, notebooks, programs, spreadsheets, compi-
> lations, recommendations, data, memoranda, and other
> documents prepared for Big Client by Circuit; and (b) any and
> all inventions which are developed and any and all improve-
> ments, implementations, developments and reductions to prac-
> tice of the subject matter performed by or for Circuit, whether
> or not patentable or copyrightable, shall be solely owned by
> Big Client and the entire right, title and interest for the United
> States and all foreign countries, shall be exclusively vested in
> Big Client. Such Services and the products or proceeds thereof
> shall be considered works made for hire and made in the
> course of the Services rendered hereunder.

They will furthermore not want to be held liable if you were
reusing a sensitive work product that you developed for another
client. Your work product must be your own work. This is normal:

> As Circuit provides the Services pursuant to this Agreement,
> all Work Product will be the original work of Circuit and its
> personnel or will be the work of third parties, which work
> Circuit has procured the right to use by or transfer to Big
> Client Entities. Circuit will not disclose to Big Client or induce
> Big Client to use the trade secrets or other confidential infor-
> mation of others.

If you believe you are developing code that you will want to reuse
at other clients (as discussed in Chapter 6), this is the clause to disagree with. This is obviously very sensitive, and your attorney
should aid you with the language in such matters.

Rates

If the client is putting rates in here, they are essentially asking
for your rate sheet (from Chapter 7). All the warnings about providing a rate sheet apply here. If asked for one, you may be getting pegged into a "contractor" hole that is inappropriate to your
concept.

To give you an idea:

> The relevant Statement of Work shall indicate whether the compensation for Circuit for the services performed by or on behalf of Circuit will be based on a fixed fee or will be based on time and materials. In either case, the per hour rate cannot exceed $200.00 per hour for Senior Data Architects and $150.00 per hour for Data Architects.

You may be tempted to agree to a staggered rate structure here with the idea that you will bill everyone at higher levels than their experience and abilities really warrant. Don't do this. If you concede a rate structure here, slot your staff into it appropriately during the SOW.

A lesser form of rate sheet is simply a maximum rate that your consultants will not exceed. While less restrictive (you may feel free to bill everyone at the maximum rate), it's nonetheless a restriction on your billing and a positioning statement that you should be comfortable with.

Liability Limits

The parties generally mutually agree to limit up to a predefined maximum the liability of the other party to them in the event of wrongdoing. This is mostly to protect the deep-pocket client. Unless you intend to make your money through the court system, limiting the client's liability to what they've paid you should be acceptable. This is one of those clauses where, usually, both parties agree to the same liability limit.

The clause is wordy, but it's something like this:

> Except for breach of Confidentiality or claims of indemnification hereunder, in no event shall a Party or its subcontractors, employees, representatives or affiliates be liable to the other Party or its subcontractors, employees, representatives or affiliates, for any consequential, indirect, punitive, incidental or special damages, whether foreseeable or unforeseeable (and whether or not the Party has been advised of the possibility of such damages), whether based upon lost goodwill, lost profits, loss of use of money, loss of data or interruption in its use or availability, stoppage of work, impairment of assets or otherwise arising out of breach of any express or implied warranty, breach of contract, negligence, misrepresentation, strict liability in tort or otherwise, and whether based on any term

in any Contract Document, any transaction performed or undertaken under or in connection with any Contract Document or otherwise. Except for breach of Confidentiality and/or claims of indemnification hereunder a Party or its subcontractors, employees, representatives or affiliates liability to the other Party and its subcontractors', employees', representatives' and subsidiaries' for damages, regardless of the form of action, shall in any event be limited to the greater of: (i) Five Hundred Thousand and 00/100 Dollars ($500,000); or (ii) the aggregate amount paid by Big Client to Circuit.

Administrivia

There are various administrivia terms that are included in most MSAs, including:

- Agreement to perform within the guidelines of the law
- Agreement that your consultants are not employees of the client in any way, shape, or form
- Agreement that the client can terminate if it goes into bankruptcy
- Agreement that the client can audit the consultancy's books with regard to their engagement
- Agreement to participate in legal defense of each other's rights
- Duration of the MSA

Finally, there will be blanket assurances that all personnel you deploy on the account will follow these terms. You may need to certify that they will have signed to the terms. Sometimes, the client will require those signed terms shared with them.

Statement of Work

Statements of work are generally originated and fully prepared by the consultant in response to client interest in receiving a work product from the consultancy. If the statement of work is a formality to tie down the agreement in writing, it could be very short, like you see in the sample in this section. If an MSA is in place with the client, the SOW would reference the MSA as containing terms that are relevant to the SOW. Without the MSA, and depending on what has been placed in the MSA, some of the terms in the MSA section could be included in the SOW. The client may want to ensure that some terms are present. Ask or be prepared for an iterative process.

It is imperative to understand the objective of the SOW—confirmation or proposal—and deliver accordingly. If it is a confirmation, the client may not appreciate the credentialing, since they may believe you are past that point in the relationship and it is unnecessary and useless information at that point.

Statement of Work

DATE August 8

Joe's Consulting
123 Main Street
New York, NY 00938

Acme Widgets
Yvonne Halford
261 Prospect Street
Boston, MA 01462

Deliverables
Two-day onsite training of Business Process Reengineering Unlimited

Project and Financial Schedule
Personnel: Joe Multicapable, President
Duration: 8/28–8/29, 2 days
Location: Onsite

Billing Schedule
Two days at @ $2,000 per day plus travel expenses

If the SOW is not simply a formality, but you are *proposing* to do work, especially if it is competitive, your SOW would contain all manner of credentialing information, not dissimilar to the RFP response material covered in Chapter 11.

Action Plan

✓ Develop with your attorney the MSA that you will use if asked, or get it from your firm.

✓ Develop one or more SOW templates with your attorney or get them from your firm.

Chapter 10

Acquiring People

- People: Who Needs Them?
- Employee Styles
- Finding People
- Action Plan

First, I want to address the maximum earning potential of a solo act in consulting, for those of you going this route. Conventional wisdom has it that the magic number is $200,000. You can slice this number down in a variety of ways. If you work full time but not more, 2,000 hours times $100 per hour is $200,000. If your bill rate is a little less, you might work a few more hours to reach $200,000. Or, you might work a bit less if your rate is higher. If your rate is much higher, it is likely that clients will look to utilize you on a shorter basis, which may leave you with some gaps in billing. Regardless, I take exception to $200,000 as an artificial limit for Jane Guru, given that our target is $500,000 gross profit. However, it's not for everyone.

Of course, there are fixed-price engagements, which involve a lot of intellectual property that can be leveraged. If you can turn a lot of these, you can certainly exceed $200,000. I discussed some of this mentality in Chapter 6, where services began to resemble software sales.

You may hear of others achieving extraordinary revenues in the area of our target $500,000 as a solo act. What is not emphasized is that these ordinarily involve not software and fixed-bid style deliveries, but a powerful presence with mass appeal that can command very high fees for services such as speaking and holding workshops. In other words, fame is the engine propelling the income. While I certainly do not discard that every reader is capable of true fame, I just want you to be discerning about the advice you receive and match it to your desired consulting profile from Chapter 1.

Even John Multicapable leverages others to get to his goals.

Most consultants will earn their $500,000 through leveraging other people on their assignments. For the Jodi Brokers and David Others of the world, utilizing other people is the business model, so this skill of acquiring people is absolutely essential. Notice that even John Multicapable is multi-capable and not relying on his own energies to get him to $500,000.

People: Who Needs Them?

There are numerous ways to utilize others in your firm and on your assignments. The way you would prefer to do it, if you have not worked in consulting, is the simple way. You will get the assignment from the client and then contract the appropriate person to the client. There will be a nice split between the bill rate and the contractor's rate. You will not have a bench.

In reality, each step in the aforementioned process is fraught with challenges, but these are exactly the challenges that Jodi Broker will overcome. First, it can be difficult to get the assignment for a person (or a project where somebody beyond yourself is required) without having people readily at your disposal, perhaps even to demonstrate and introduce to the prospect to secure considera-tion. Many clients ask for resumes very early in the process. If you are starting from scratch, without bench or without warm and relevant consultants you can show off, you may have to work extra hard just to get the assignments.

The other side of that coin is the challenge involved in staffing that assignment. Without employees or a network, although you can rely on your talents to find people, the problems are that (1) it takes time; (2) it's likely competitive, which means that the client is soliciting other firms; and (3) consultants without a track record with you will not trust that you really have the assignment, and they are likewise considering competitive offers.

John Multicapable and David Others will utilize some employees in the process by hiring some people who fit the assignments they have and are targeting. They will then have some people who they can control in the sense of assignment. Employees will not take another assignment and leave you at the altar (except when they quit the firm).

The strength of your consultant net-work is key to the Jodi Broker strategy. This is why it is something that tends to build over the years.

As to that rich split that you are seeking, if you are starting from scratch, clients will be giving you "prove it" bill rates to work with, and consultants will be giving you "prove it" pay rates to work with.

The key to success is the network. And you will not be able to keep a robust network in your head. You will need a system. I refer to some contact management software later in the book, but it is useful for both clients/prospects as well as resources. There are more robust web-based software-as-a-service solutions, such as salesforce.com, that are fee-based by the month. When there are multiple people in your firm seeking clients and resources, you may find that the offline synchronization features of PC-based software are inadequate for keeping you all up to date and off of each other's toes.

A lot of this chapter involves putting the shoe on the other foot—putting the consultant into the position of hiring other consultants. Sometimes this will happen to a consultant in conjunction with being contracted by another consulting firm. Deal-making abilities that work for all (and foremost the clients!) are essential.

With a network, Jodi Broker will be able to create competition for the assignment at the consultant level. If one consultant's rates would leave her with an unacceptable $5/hour margin, she can potentially find someone else who will do the job.[1] She will also have more options for presentation to the client.

For positioning reasons, a lot of consulting firms do not tout that they provide people, even though I discussed it as a basic service in Chapter 6. Notice I did not say that they *don't* provide people. Most do, regardless of whether they promote it. You can decide whether you want to promote that service. The fear is that you will be viewed alongside the multitude of firms who are "body shoppers" doing low-value-added resume keyword matching for low-level positions. If that is the business you are interested in, I can tell you that surely there are some who do it very well and prosper. When I suggest that a consultant provide people, they are targeted, known people in a discipline the firm understands. Hence, the network!

As to whether to hire the resources as employees or utilize them in a contract capacity, the key question here is obviously, "Do you have enough business to keep them utilized?" You will gain a higher split from employees on billing than you will from independent consultants. However, there comes the potential for downtime.[2] Most David Others and John Multicapable consultancies have about a 70/30 ratio between employee consultants and outside contractors.

The number-one point of consternation for a growing consultancy is when to hire. It is an ongoing tough decision point.

Hopefully, this book is providing you with information on what to do with some employee downtime. It is unethical to hire consultants, who aren't expected to sell business, and terminate their employment the first non-billing week. If you call what you run a business—and you must if you are hiring people—you simply have to have productive "bench time" activities.

---

[1]With a 30-percent split as the target.
[2]Don't forget to factor benefits and downtime into the employee-cost equation.

Employee Styles

If you are part of a large consultancy, it is well established that you will grow through others. However, regardless of how you establish the professional employee arrangement you will use to utilize others in the practice, there are numerous ways to engage them.

Regular Salary

This describes those who are not in a temporary status and who are regularly scheduled to work a fulltime schedule. Generally, they are eligible for a benefits package. These are the people you hire and grow around. It is my belief that the best kinds of people for a small practice are those who are able to do a variety of activities necessary for clients, including sales and sales support. Phil Simon calls them "hybrids," as discussed in the "Finding and Retaining Hybrids" sidebar a bit later in this chapter.

Pay strategy for your regular, salaried employees is important to think about as well, even in the first 90 days. You could adopt a large-consultancy mindset and have strict definitions for each level of employee regarding roles and responsibilities, salary grades, and titles. Others will adopt a more freestyle attitude toward this subject.

You want to fill your employee ranks with experienced people with multiple capabilities and contract the rest, unless you are firmly focused and gaining contracts around services that need specific skills. Usually, if the client cares about who specifically someone is, it is your senior resources. If clients care whether your resources are employees, they will prefer them to be firm employees. Interestingly, I have not found a pattern within client profiles as to whether or not they care. It seems to be an individual decision. Large and small companies alike may or may not care about that aspect of the relationship. To me, it's somewhat important. However, more important would be the relationship itself: Does the consulting firm really know the people it is putting forward?

These experienced people you hire have needs that don't always fit nicely into a box. Some want to be assured of local clientele and minimize their traveling. Others are mercenaries[3] who want

---

[3] I mean this in a good sense!

every dollar they can achieve as quickly as possible and are willing to work around the clock. Others want the dollars but are not willing to pay the price. Finally, others want to practice a specific skill set or work on a particular technology. Their interests and abilities need to provide enough flexibility across the spectrum of client engagements you are likely to get to make it worthwhile for you.

You can meter your downside (and upside) with some variable-based pay. You can pay employee consultants a mix of a healthy base with an upside according to performance, which may come from a mix of billing hours, client satisfaction, adding credibility to the firm, and helping bring in new business.

> **NOTE**
> Some want a large upside—in other words, part ownership. While you don't necessarily have to make them a partner (see Chapter 15), you can also use company equity as a means of payment. Only use company equity if the person is a true "game changer" for the firm. This means she *must* be able to bring in business, not just deliver on it. Even with that expectation, meter out the equity in "prove it" increments.

Because of the flexibility desired by senior consultants who you may hire and the variable nature of the pay, I recommend a less rigid structure for titles, roles/responsibilities, and pay.

Regular Hourly

This describes those who are not in a temporary status and who are regularly scheduled to work a fulltime schedule. Generally, they are eligible for benefits, except for PTO and holiday pay.

Part-Time

This describes those who are not assigned to a temporary status and who work continuously for a specified number of hours per week that is less than 40 hours. Part-time employees receive all legally mandated benefits (such as Social Security and workers' compensation insurance). One may be considered a part-time employee yet still be eligible for certain benefits.

Every consultancy I know of has had difficulties managing their workforce. Though you may have gotten the person gainfully employed—or contracted, as the case may be—over time, it is human nature to ask, "What have you done for me lately?" That is the question that both parties need to be prepared to continually address.

Temporary

This describes those who are hired as interim replacements, to temporarily supplement the workforce, or to assist in the completion of a specific project. Employment assignments in this category are of a limited duration. Employment beyond any initially stated period does not in any way imply a change in employment status. Temporary employees retain that status unless and until notified of a change. While temporary employees receive all legally mandated benefits (such as workers' compensation insurance and Social Security), they are ineligible for all of other benefits.

Per Diem

This describes those who routinely work either a full time or a part-time schedule and who accept additional compensation in lieu of participation in all but legally mandated benefit programs. You offer this category in limited classifications and to limited numbers of employees. Employment in this category cannot be credited in any way toward any benefit program, even if the employee is later assigned to a benefit-eligible category.

Casual

This describes those who have established an employment relationship with you but who are assigned to work on an intermittent basis. While they receive all legally mandated benefits, they are ineligible for all other benefits.

Regardless of whether one of the employee arrangements mentioned in this chapter is utilized or whether you are engaging the person as a contractor, it is important to get to know the person before presentation. Ideally, this comes in the form of actual work experience with the person. However, that could limit your universe substantially, which is where Step 2, "friends of friends," comes in. Ask your warm network who they have worked with and who worked out well.

What you are trying to get to—without getting too many layers removed—is someone who has worked with someone who you ultimately know to have done good work. LinkedIn is a marvelous tool for finding people who are linked to someone and who may know their work or know someone for you.

FINDING AND RETAINING HYBRIDS

From *Why New Systems Fail: Theory and Practice Collide* by Phil Simon (AuthorHouse, 2009)

Consulting firms hire and train new consultants at considerable costs. It typically takes freshly hired consultants anywhere from three to six months to gain certification and become proficient enough with a product to guide clients effectively through an implementation, although some take quite a bit longer. After this period, consultancies rightfully expect a return on their investment—i.e., consultants need to start billing clients as soon as possible. After obtaining their certifications, consultants should not expect to attend additional training sessions. Down the road, ambitious consultants may have opportunities to expand their skill sets. However, in the short- and near-terms, it is not reasonable for consultancies to produce "techno-functional" super-users.

While consultancies place a great deal of emphasis on billing, the individual consultant typically possesses a tremendous desire to maximize bonuses. Such bonuses are almost always tied to utilization. In tandem, these incentives tend to create consultants with a great deal of depth in an individual application but not nearly as much breadth. A GL consultant at a large firm, for example, may know invoice matching inside and out but know very little about fixed asset management. Alternatively, many payroll consultants know a great deal about how the application processes paychecks but nothing about the fields and tables updated by each payroll program in the process.

Let's look at an example at one organization with a traditional, purely functional payroll consultant (Donna) interacting with the client's designated report developer (Sam):

- The payroll manager (Anna) needs a custom report from the new system.
- Donna creates the reporting specification for Anna, leaving out key technical pieces of information.
- Sam attempts to create the report but cannot without additional information. He emails Donna.
- Donna receives the email but is fully engaged in system testing. She is unable to answer Sam's questions for three days.
- Donna asks Anna to elaborate on the reporting requirements.

- Donna finally provides the information to Sam, who then creates a template of the report and sends an example to Donna.
- Donna reviews the report with Anna and makes some changes.
- Frustrated, Sam receives the changes requested and has to re-create the report because it contains tables and joins that make the original version of the report useless.
- After a month of back and forth, the report is ready for Anna to sign off.

This is hardly an ideal process, especially if the report is essential and the project is running behind schedule. Now, let's look at the same process spearheaded by Pete, a highly skilled functional consultant with extensive experience in Crystal Reports:

- Anna needs the same report.
- Pete asks Anna specifically what is required, already thinking about the required tables and fields.
- Pete knows that the number and size of the required tables will cause this report to take six hours to complete soon after the client goes live; he does not even attempt to build the report using the traditional tables because he knows that the effort is futile.
- Pete quickly puts together a formal reporting specification and creates a custom view in the database that aggregates this information. He provides the code for this view to the IT department for sign off.
- Pete creates the report and provides Anna with a sample.
- The report is spot-on and takes minutes to run. Anna signs off on it immediately.

Now, multiply this process by 50—a conservative estimate of the number of custom reports typically required by a client during an implementation. Isn't the hybrid consultant worth 20 percent more?

An organization's desire to keep initially expected consulting costs at a minimum often results in its staffing projects with consultants who wear only one hat. An independent's rate may exceed another's by a considerable margin, but brings a great deal more to the table. Depending on the role required, hybrid consultants are almost always well worth their premiums. Organizations that utilize hybrids tend to reduce total consulting expenses.

However, the day will come—and possibly early on when you're starting out—when you will need to talk to strangers. You might meter back some of this due diligence for people you already know; however, you can always say that you put everyone through the gauntlet.[4]

What should an interview consist of that is outside of the normal bounds? Well, first of all, with busy schedules and people widespread, you will need to learn to do some of this remotely. Try GoToMeeting, Skype, or another instant messenger webcam for the visual effects.

What's new and different about your consulting interview? Well, in addition to the usual stuff, since communication is so important, I would add submitting a writing sample to be reviewed, giving a presentation, reviewing a case study that you present the person with (ahead of time is okay), and performing a behavioral interview. Once again, I turn to Phil Simon for information (in the following sidebar) about the behavioral interview.

BEHAVIORAL INTERVIEWS

From *Why New Systems Fail: Theory and Practice Collide* by Phil Simon (AuthorHouse, 2009)

How can an organization guarantee that it is hiring a true system expert? In short, it cannot. There is no scientific way of determining expertise in an application. One method that should weed out "posers" is the behavioral interview. In this type of interview, the interviewer asks the applicant a question, such as, "Tell me about a specific challenge that you faced on an implementation."

The interviewer should tell the applicant to frame responses in terms of three things:

■ The background or situation establishing the issue
■ The tasks or actions that the individual took to resolve that issue, not the team
■ The outcome or results of those actions

A useful acronym for behavioral interviews is STAR: Situation, Task/Action, and Result. Consider the following two responses from Ronnie and Ricky:

Comparison of Applicant Responses in Behavioral Interview

	Ronnie	*Ricky*
Situation	As we were about to go live with SAP, I discovered a data issue with a key financial conversion program.	We had problems with SAP as we were about to go live.

---

[4] *If* you do—tell the truth!

Task/Action	I alerted senior management of the issue and researched the options. I wrote extensive queries isolating the suspect data and distributed it to end-users, emphasizing the need for immediate action. I coordinated the validation of that data. Also, I found a patch on the support site and alerted the IT manager, who installed it in a TEST data area. I tested the patch and determined that it resolved the issue. I recommended that it should be applied to the PROD data area.	IT handled the issue. I kept people informed.
Result	The patch resolved the issue. We activated the system as scheduled.	The patch resolved the issue. We activated the system as scheduled.

Note how Ronnie can articulate the specific actions that he took to identify and resolve the problem. Ricky can only speak in general terms about the problem and its resolution. As such, Ricky appears to be an inferior candidate. At this point, [the interviewer] should ensure that Ronnie's references check out.

In behavioral interviews, the outcome of a situation is not nearly as important as the steps taken by each individual in response to that situation. The applicant who did everything possible to resolve an issue may not have been able to save the day, through no fault of her own. Conversely, the individual who acted as though "things would work themselves out" may have been right. More than the outcome, the interviewer should look for what each applicant did and did not do in response to the problem.

Finding People

Finding people is not really the problem. Being mindful and tracking them is the problem. If you are active in your field, you will naturally come across many prospective useful people. Most will be gainfully employed. It doesn't matter. Keep track of them in your system.

Conference attendance and speaking greatly increases your touch points, and certainly if you exercise the process described in this chapter when you are searching for a specific person (asking friends of friends, and so on), you will expand your network.

In Chapter 4, I talked about brokers and online contract job boards. Well, now the shoe is on the other foot, and you are the one on the other side of the ad looking for people to extend your capabilities. Job boards are a last resort, and you will work much harder at them to get a similar result than you will by utilizing your network. However, when you're pressed for time and need to try anything and everything, they are there. Just be sure to do the due diligence described in this chapter for them.

Action Plan

✓ Begin a tracking system for potential resources.

✓ Design the style and pay plan you will begin discussions with for your potential employee hires.

✓ Design your interview approach.

Chapter 11

Requests for Information/
Requests for Proposals

- When to Respond
- What's in an RFP?
- RFP Timelines
- Action Plan

Companies will issue formal requests and sometimes invite anybody and everybody to respond. Requests for information (RFI) are used to cull the field down to those organizations they may wish to take the process further with, possibly to a request for proposals (RFP). An RFP is a little more committal than a request for information. The idea behind an RFP is that there will be a consultancy selection contract award at the end of the process.

These definitions are only guidelines based on the seeming convergence in the use of the terms. In reality, consistency and the linear nature of one of these requests of any kind is merely a façade. Governmental RFPs tend to hold true to the outlines of the timelines in the RFP, but other organizations do not necessarily.

The issuing company holds most of the cards in this process. If you receive an RFI/RFP, you need to decide whether you are going to participate. Additionally, if you are time constrained, you may decide the level of commitment you are going to make to the process. However, usually these are highly competitive, and anything less than a pretty full commitment will not win the day.

As with many of the activities in this book necessary to run a firm or a practice, what is at stake is your time. Repeated efforts and mental energy toward activities that do not eventually bear revenue fruit will kill the practice. So, do I only recommend you participate in those RFPs that are winnable? Usually, yes, but not necessarily... Let me explain.

In the first 90 days of your consulting, you will likely have no material built for responding to proposals. Eventually, depending on your business model, you may need such material. We'll talk more about writing in Chapter 13, "Writing and Speaking," but be sure that writing skills and writing needs do not stop with writing for general audiences in the form of articles and so on. Heck, it doesn't even begin there. Remember the website content you formed in Chapter 3? That was some writing. However, much of what goes on websites is very "glossy" in nature—highly abbreviated sloganeering and general-purpose condensed paragraphs. In RFPs,[1] you will need to delve into more detail and quite possibly address some very specific questions.

---

[1] I'll use the term RFPs, but these references refer to RFIs as well.

You may want to participate in some unwinnable RFPs in the early days to experience the process and force the development of some material that may be reused on future, winnable requests. You may get lucky and win. You may also gain the attention of the client for something in the future that may make more sense for you because of your specific focus.

On the flip side, after 10 to 15 response cycles, if you've catalogued your response material well, it may be a fairly simple matter to respond. Again, the downside is your time. You may have bench consultants or warm outside consultants who could put it together as well. If it's something you can provide client value for, you may win, and if a lot of your time is not required, there is little reason not to respond.

When to Respond

Some key criteria for determining whether the request is winnable are:

- Who is this going to? The more, the less merry for you. Stay away from "cattle calls" where everybody and their grandmother is invited to respond.[2]

- Why me/us? How did the client select you to receive it? If you were picked due to specific qualifications you may have, or you seem to meet some criteria they have for selection, that is good. If you were picked because you are a consultancy or you were in a list of 100 firms they found somewhere on the Web (all of which were invited), that is not a good sign. This may go without saying, but seeking out general RFPs or pulling them off the Web is not a good idea.

- Is the RFP full of boilerplate questions? If the question list reads like a laundry list with lots of material you can't see why the client needs answered, it's not a good sign that the client will actually be able to make a decision. Conversely, they may have already made up their mind and are just going through the motions of the RFP to satisfy a requirement or demonstrate false diligence. This happens much more often than you might think.

---

[2]Imagine the waste of the client's time in reading all the submissions—*if* they even do!

- Does is appear that the real winner has been predetermined (and it's not you)? It's not only boilerplate questions that indicate you are being used—you may get some believable information that indicates the jig is up and the determination has been done. The biggest red flag I've found is lack of communication.

- Are the questions general or specific? Succinct, focused questions for which you immediately know the answer for your firm.

- Is the RFP targeting what you do well? So many clients do not know the difference between what you do and what they are asking for, despite it being glaringly obvious to you that it's a mismatch. Sure, you can stretch at this point. Just make sure you can follow through in the next round when you are asked for more information.

- Does the opportunity seem to be profitable? If the RFP is full of language of concern about your rates and reminders of the bad economy we're in or how conservative the company is when it comes to paying consultants, this could be an RFP that, once won, is more trouble than it's worth to the bottom line.

They key question to ask in terms of fit is, "Will you be able to deliver the client superior value if you were to win this RFP?" If not, don't bother responding. Too many consultancies teach their new consultants *how* to sell, not *when* to sell.

You should *never* respond to an RFP without some interaction with the client. If you cannot get the interaction, and you cannot get your answers, then it is almost surely unwinnable. It may be a cattle call, or it may be a sucker play.

The government is where the RFP originated, and that is the mentality many firms take on when they issue their RFPs. Governments are notorious for having exactly the wrong answers you are seeking to almost every criteria question. They send huge[3] RFPs to everyone they can find who can spell something or another. I think their RFPs are an aggregation of all previous RFPs plus a few new questions or twists on existing questions. Regulations force some of this on them. However, to their credit, they do seem to read the responses and stick fairly close to their stated timetables.

I'm not a big fan of RFPs as being a good idea for clients. I'm much bigger on the client developing relationships with their consultancies, learning what a good fit is for both, and acting accordingly. I believe clients get more value from doing more upfront

---

[3]How about 250-page huge? I've gotten a few in that range!

self-study and then some active discovery with prospective consulting organizations, as opposed to sending out RFPs blindly to lists. Clients might spend five times as long doing RFPs, as opposed to relationship building, to get to the same selection result. However, the RFP may be the only palatable thing inside the company structure to show diligence. It also puts the ball quickly into the hands of the consultants.

Many clients do not even have any idea who is receiving the RFP. And I don't mean they don't really know the consultancy they're sending it to; I mean they don't even know their name. How could that be? Easy—they utilize a consultancy to *write* the RFP and manage the process. Your response could be going to that consultancy (imagine the library of response material they're building) and not to the end client. Sometimes that consultancy is prohibited from participating in the RFP, and sometimes not.

You cannot blame a client for asking (anything)!

LESSONS LEARNED

There is a company I pass on the way to the airport, so consequently I pass it a lot. This company is one of several who taught me some lessons for which I am now grateful. My heartburn at this company has subsided over the years, but I recall distinctly receiving a three-firm targeted RFP. Signs were good at first. I went in to get more detailed requirements (so they were talking to me early on!). Then, the more I got into my response and had questions, the less in touch they were—until we had achieved radio silence.

I foolishly put in tens of hours under deadline and at the peril of other business—*after* the last communication from the client toward winning the RFP. I submitted it with the full expectation of not just having it read, but of actually winning. Not only did we not win, I couldn't even get the client to tell me we didn't win. That's how silent they were. I was never passed upwards in the organization to meet with the real decision makers (another warning sign), but when I bypassed my contact and went to these people, they were downright hostile about spending any time with me (after I spent about 50 hours on the RFP). They probably slipped when they said they had made their decision weeks ago. Gee, thanks for the letting me know! I almost picketed the place after that.

If you ever wonder why consultant fees are so high, it's partly because we have to make up for the time we lose and waste on situations like this!

These warning signs about the winnability of RFPs usually are staring you in the face. I guess consultants are optimists, because it doesn't seem to stop many.

When they are not, that would be a red flag to you. If an organization writes the RFP, they can easily gear the questions toward what they are good at. And furthermore, they have already passed a gate with the client—they are working there! It will be somewhat easier for the client to keep the relationship going into the actual project. Often, when the consultancy who wrote the RFP is participating in the response, it is one of those sucker plays.

What's in an RFP?

If you are still wondering what kinds of things would be asked for in an RFP over and above your resumes, believe me, there is a lot. Strategic and project consulting is crucial to the success of clients, and they want to be sure they make the right decision. One of the first things you will notice is that they ask for many things they already know and that are readily available from the information you've already given them or your website.

Well, guess what? Rather than pore through your website and your materials, they want to get the responses into a common format so they can compare you all side by side—apples to apples.

Selection criteria are sometimes revealed to the bidders, but sometimes they are not. I am referring to the ranking of the various components of the RFP. For example:

In terms of how to answer each question, the answer is truthfully and from the heart, yet assertively. Each question contains knock-out criteria whereby the client is looking for reasons to eliminate you from the process.

The degree to which the proposed system satisfies the business requirements and management process	10%
Overall system functionality, flexibility, ease of use, and performance	20%
Support and training provided for implementation	30%
Initial product cost and ongoing license and maintenance costs	20%
Ongoing maintenance and training	5%
Corporate financial condition	15%

Sometimes the client does not know their selection process going into the RFP process. This is definitely something you should ask about—so you know where to focus your energies if possible—but it's not necessary for a winnable RFP. I've seen several RFPs for which the predefined selection criteria were thrown out the window during the process because the client fell in love with one of the bidders, who ended up being lower in the selection criteria results.

Here is a sample RFP outline:

Much of the information is devoted to explaining the work that the client needs done. To do that, the environment has to be explained as well. This is all good, because you will need as much of this information as you can get in order to respond appropriately. There are also terms and conditions and response instructions. You will want to absorb all of this information. Sometimes there is an unusual nugget in there that will affect your response (for example, the client will provide the database administration).

The costs, effort, and energy for providing the response is on you. Occasionally, the RFP itself will state this. You are not being forced to reply, and if you find the RFP amusing, ridiculous, abusive, in poor taste, grammatically challenged, lacking enough information,[4] or needlessly overdone, you can opt out.[5] There

---

[4]If the RFP is explicitly asking for a fixed bid, there needs to be a lot of information—or a path to obtaining that information. Refer to Chapter 7 for a discussion of fixed-bid work.

[5]I've tried to "consult" the clients in this case about what is best for them (in my opinion, of course) in writing effective RFPs, but to no avail. After writing and issuing an RFP, they will usually stand behind it as is.

may also be terms and conditions relating to how to respond,[6] that the client is under no obligations, that the client will not return your materials, and so on.

Then begins the series of questions to which you must respond (the "Proposal of Bidders" section in the sample RFP outline). This can go anywhere the client wants it to. They will ask questions about the size of your firm, the projects you have participated in, sales levels, offices, service offerings, technology specializations, and so on.

Your approach to the problem, methodology, and project plan may be up next. This is where you could get into a ton of wasted hours. The client asking you for a project plan may have you double- and triple-checking your winnability factor. Either way, provide value and show experience, but don't let it run away. This section will be completely contextual to your discipline, so there's not a lot more I can say about it that would apply to all readers. To give you a flavor, though, here are some sample questions:

- Describe your approach for supporting polyhierarchical taxonomies.

- Describe your ability to easily manage the exchange of metadata among tools using corporately accepted standard data exchange formats.

- Describe how you minimize the redundancy of metadata stored by multiple tools.

Oh yes, then the resumes of people you intend to put on the project (or at least in the key roles) and references may be requested.

Then, finally, is the section where you outline your project costs. Normally, you like to know before you go to a great deal of effort whether the client is into paying your level of rates (whatever they may be). Do they expect to pay $60 an hour for a database administrator when you are thinking $150? However, that information is scant in an RFP. This is a very difficult aspect of an RFP to understand. About the best gauge is just knowing who else is responding and how they respond to this question. Firms like yours will charge similar rates. If you're a global, well-known, multinational firm, rates are among the highest.

Clients don't often realize (and can't articulate it if they do) that the client's business and political environment plays a large role in a consultant's response and in client success.

I just can't get out of the realm of advice to clients when it comes to writing RFPs. Okay, so, clients, does it matter if a (large) firm has done 300 similar projects if the people you will be getting on your project have a collective one similar project under their belt? Biasing the RFP toward the large firm may hurt the client's ability to make the best selection.

If you haven't noticed, I am continually emphasizing that your time is your most valuable asset.

Don't overuse your references on fishing expeditions. They are busy, and despite loving you, they will soon grow tired of the calls.

---

[6]This can run the gamut from freeform responses to multiple-choice responses.

> **NOTE**
>
> A sign of a client that may not yet know what they are looking for—and therefore may delay or cancel their decision—is the inclusion of firms from vastly different profiles in the responding list. Global, multinational firms, boutique firms, the consulting arms of software and hardware vendor firms, H1B-focused bodyshops,[7] and outsourcing firms will approach a problem with some pretty different mindsets and solutions.

RFP Timelines

Timelines are included in RFPs and should be adhered to by all respondents, even though the client will potentially miss their dates and occasionally scuttle the whole thing. Here is an example timeline for an RFP:

Release RFP	2/8
Email-only question-and-answer period	3/1
Closure date for supplier proposal	3/1
Review of supplier proposal completed	3/15
Preferred suppliers notified	3/16
Unsuccessful suppliers notified	3/16
Bidder conference	3/21
Presentations	3/25
Supplier selection	3/29
Work begins	4/5

What you see here is typical. Once you receive the RFP, you have three weeks to formulate your questions and email them to the company. Keep in mind that answers to questions from all participants will go out to all participants. Other bidders can utilize your questions as tips for how they may respond to the RFP. If it is not evident in the RFP itself, one of the questions to ask is, "Who is this RFP going to?" You may not be able to ask personal questions, such as, "Why did we receive this RFP?" in the question-and-answer period. The answer to the question of how many firms received the RFP may provide you with some clues

---

[7]This is just an example. Just because a firm uses H1B personnel does not make the firm a bodyshop.

there. Remember, if you cannot get satisfactory answers to the basic questions, the contract is likely unwinnable.

On 3/16 in the sample timeline, the preferred and unsuccessful suppliers are notified. This is called a *down-selection* or *short-listing* because some suppliers are eliminated at this point, but more than one remains in the running. The client will then have a bidder conference, which is usually held at their site with all bidders and is an opportunity to interact with the client all at once, drilling in on some questions. The client may reveal some things only during the bidder conference. And while it's important to listen to the client at the conference, it is also important to listen to the competition present at the bidder conference.

Finally, on 3/25, this client is asking for presentations from all of those on the short list. That's the final gate to final selection on 3/29. Then you need to mobilize to begin on 4/5.

If this sounds like a lot of work, it is! If this sounds equivalent to picking a horse to win a horse race or rolling the dice in Vegas hoping for a 7...well, then, you are not thinking of using RFPs strategically. Winnable RFPs can be a nice addition to your arsenal. However, blindly pursuing any and all RFPs and making them the focus of the practice is a mistake. Building relationships with clients, being selectively invited to RFPs, and selectively accepting them can be great ways to win your large deals, which many will need to get into the $500,000 gross profit level.

Action Plan

Seek out some RFPs in your space. You do not necessarily have to bid on them (or you may), but at least you can get a feel for what some in your field may look like so you can begin thinking about gaining the experience and the response information necessary to be a successful bidder one day.

Chapter 12

Client Communications

Time management may be the biggest factor in enabling one to become a sustainable consultant, but communication with clients is what separates the levels of consultants. Even if you're a deep technician in your concept, well before you get your hands on the keyboard, there is the matter of understanding what needs to be done. And afterwards, there is the matter of communicating what you did. Almost every aspect of consulting involves communication. It merits a special focus.

The consultant's communication philosophy should emphasize honesty and frequency.

In this chapter, I am focused less on the written and spoken word that goes out to a mass audience or in contract form for a predetermined purpose. That will be addressed in the next chapter, as well as somewhat in the chapters on RFPs, contracts, and partnerships. I firmly believe that wherever you are with communications, you can improve quickly. I have seen it happen repeatedly that this is an area where people—consultants and clients—can learn to improve through focus and practice. Indeed, I find that in my consulting to clients, helping them become as effective as they can be as individuals as quickly as possible, I naturally gravitate to sharing communication skills. I will do that now, from the perspective of the consultant in a project.

Communication Should Be Honest

Most of the time when a consultant says a client is unreasonable, you can trace it back to a lack of communication on the part of the consultant!

An old model of consulting is to keep the bad and the undesirable out of the face of the client by sheltering the client from them. I've seen much whitewashing of true project status go on all around me with clients. It may work for a while, like expedient approaches do, but eventually it is crippling to the relationship. There are myriad irrelevant reasons at this point in the project as to why reality is lagging expectations. Early communication of issues and resetting expectations creatively and in conjunction with the client helps alleviate compounding the problem. However, all honest communication is not done in the face of crisis, and not all projects will fall behind expectations, and this is certainly not the formula for your consulting success. It can take work to be a completely honest communicator in any environment.

Listen First

Your existence at a client is to meet and exceed their expectations. Meeting expectations begins by setting them. That process begins by understanding them. The client could be underestimating or overestimating your capabilities or, more likely, the capability of any consulting team to deliver. You should know more about what can be done with your discipline than your client, but the client knows their environment, their organizational politics, their skeletons, and their personal standards best. This is extremely valuable input because a project can be estimated at plus or minus 50-percent work effort based on client environmental factors. Working together with the client, a project can be sized appropriately.

You don't need to under-promise. Accurately promise.

Being a good listener is very difficult for many consultants because they are used to giving the communication, and they lack the necessary patience to hear others out. Most of us have to work on this. Active listening does not have to be boring to you, however. It takes effort to shape the communication toward what interests you as well as effort to get over the idea that you can only focus on exciting subject matter.

I am, for example, passionately interested in learning—a trait of many good consultants. If I'm learning, I'm completely happy. So, I put the client in the position of educator and me in the position of student. I ask questions that I really care about the answer to—either because I care deeply about project success, because I enjoy learning, or, as is usually the case in client communication, both. This communication is not dull.

The key factor to better communications may be *energy*. It does take energy to be alert enough to listen effectively. I found it important enough to take a special focus in Chapter 2 on health, which systemically leads to better energy. If you're not able to walk away feeling like you've comprehended what the client has said, consider whether you are engaged with sufficient energy.

> **NOTE**
> In my early days of strategy consulting, I engaged too much in the "drop paper" mentality, where I would develop the strategy or other deliverable and deliver it as if the client would read it, comprehend it, and know what to do with it. Wrong! No deliverable is complete without client corroboration, which only occurs when the client cries "Uncle" about your communication.

Dealing in less interesting subject matter? Take notes, because you're more likely to forget the less interesting. The act of writing also contributes to retention.

If you're outcome-centric, as many consultants are, consider a desired, ongoing mini-outcome to be the ability to recap conversations later. That is, you are looking for the key message that the client expresses in the communication. Make sure you walk away knowing this message. It is not a bad idea to document the key messages, which does the most good if you can locate the notes later. This means applying some level of organization to your notetaking.

Finally, avoid contentious-sounding talk and especially email. Being outright rude is one thing, but good consultants are never that. They can, however, fall into the trap of conveying the wrong message with the use of their words.

Different cultural backgrounds are one contributor to miscommunication. Another is expediency, which leads to lazy communication. Consultants who have not politically mapped the organization (and some who have) are often dancing around landmines they are unaware of. Expressing from your point of view is a good way for consultants to acknowledge the complexity of the environment. This means communicating with phrases such as, "In my opinion," "I've observed," "I believe," "I feel," and the like. In truth, you are always coming from your point of view, so this is just honest.

Communication Should Be Frequent

Higher-value consultants are those able and willing to engage in communication with the client and not just be buried on the project team and kept away from client personnel.

Without being overbearing and unfocused, communication with the client should occur to the point of the client letting you know that she has heard enough. That being said, communication should be purposeful. Clients who seem to *like* to hibernate from the details need communication as much as those who like to know every little detail. Each requires a focused strategy. For the hibernators, the consultant will need to be especially diligent about structured communication and seek out the client. For the involved client (which clients have every right to be), opportunities are ample. The goal may be to communicate confidence in the process, especially if the client is being overbearing and detracting from your ability to meet deadlines.

Structured Project Communication

Consultants in short or multi-month engagements should make it a point to deliver a weekly project status. Although that format could take on multiple forms, I have found that something containing the following elements is essential (for one person or a team delivery):

- Project objectives
- Project success criteria
- Project milestones and milestone status
- Changes to milestones and their dates since the last report
- Activities and accomplishments since the last report
- Planed activities for the next week
- Needs from the client

A sample weekly status report is shown on the next page.

The point of listing project objectives and success criteria (you do have them, right?) up front and center is to serve as a visible reminder of the agreed obligation. Too many projects break down because the consulting team loses focus about why it is there in the first place. When this is obvious to the client, it will be hard for them to have confidence in the work product.

Eventually, client deliverables must be codified into projects. This leads us to the "on time, on budget" aspect of the status report. Any multi-month delivery comes with key interim deliverables. These are breadcrumbs that lead to the on-time, on-budget overall project. You should definitely know enough about any discipline for which you are delivering a project to break it down into milestones. I cannot imagine you would win the project business otherwise.

Despite what you may hear, nothing has or will replace being on time and on budget as the most important criteria in delivering a project for a client.

> **NOTE**
> In an NBA basketball game, scores and game clocks are not kept in the referee's head. He does not suddenly blow the whistle and say, "Game over! Suns win 104 to 99. Goodbye." The time and the score are kept on large scoreboards for all to see throughout the game. Do you have a scoreboard for your client? It is important to know how much progress is being made throughout the NBA game and throughout a project.

To: Client Representative

From: William McKnight

Re: Status of Business Process Reengineering Project through 11/25

Objectives

■ To be listed here

Success Criteria

■ To be listed here

Project Milestones

Ref	What	Date	Status

Milestone Dates That Have Changed Since Last Week, If Any

Ref	Old Date	New Date	Reason

Project Activities and Accomplishments This Period

■ To be listed here

Other Points of Note This Week

■ To be listed here

Planned Activities

Ref	Who	What	By When	Status

Needs to Make Planned Activities Happen

■ To be listed here

The point of listing the milestones up front is also to keep them front and center. Milestones are more likely to change than project objectives and success criteria, so I have a section to call out those changes—and the reasons why. You usually have the latitude to make small changes, such as one to three weeks, to the milestones. These are usually pretty explainable and understandable. However, any time you are extending key dates, it requires conversation. One date change that usually necessitates extended discussion with the client is the final project delivery date.

Nothing in the status report should constitute what the client would view as a large negative surprise. Unstructured forms of communication—discussions, working meetings, email, phone calls, and so on—should have taken care of this as soon as the issue was realized.

Recent and upcoming activities are the meaty part of the status report and perhaps the most interesting to the client (assuming milestone dates didn't change). The Needs to Make Planned Activities Happen section of the report is your opportunity to document what *you* expect from the client. Even if it has been communicated otherwise (and it should be), document it here, because conversations and emails tend to get lost over time. Project status reports should tell the story of the project as it progresses week to week.

You cannot depend on status reports to necessarily be read, let alone comprehended. Plus, if communication is as important as I say it is, you will want to utilize multiple channels. You can emphasize the channel that works best, but I would not discount a true status report and status meetings. A weekly status meeting (or call), ideally the day following status report distribution, is an opportunity to read the report together, ensure communication, fill in all gaps, and make progress on the real project issues.

Simply getting everybody in a room is not communication.

A project should also generate numerous bits of documentation. This will be very specific to the type of project, but generally there is design documentation, requirements, interview notes and meeting minutes, architecture diagrams, project plans, organizational charts, process documentation, technical specifications, training documentation, guiding principles, support plans, migrations plans, and so on. There is also documentation collected from the client that is interesting to the entire team or that you may want to document that you are investing your faith into. For example, if the client gives you a technical specification that you are using to make decisions, you will want to document that fact so both you and the client know which specification is being used as the assumptive truth.

All of this electronic documentation should be collected in a common place, such as a file folder, an intranet site, or a collaboration tool such as the popular Microsoft SharePoint.

The idea is not for the consultant to live with the project forever. Clients are usually smart and can see through cheap efforts to create an addiction to your services beyond which they anticipated. The better route is to do an exceptional job, which gives you authority to do more projects for that client, get a reference, and so on.

A final aspect of structured communications is knowledge transfer. Although there are serious informal aspects to this, usually specific steps—again appropriate to the project—should be baked into the project for the purpose of ensuring that they happen. The idea behind knowledge transfer is to communicate to the client what they need to ensure all your efforts are not lost when you leave. This may include some formal training toward the end of the project. It may also include developing the documentation necessary to upgrade, enhance, migrate,[1] and otherwise fully utilize toward future goals the work that you are doing for them. If it's relevant (for example, you developed computer code for the client), the client should have the documentation so that a skilled resource can, if necessary, reverse-engineer the work product to do said enhancements.

Clients will tend to underestimate the serious maintenance needs of consultant projects. True consultative consultants will explain this to the client carefully. You should consider your responsibilities to the project to continue well beyond your final day on the project.

Political Sustainability of Work Product

Perhaps nowhere is communication more important than in garnering political sustainability for your project. This refers to keeping it alive and progressing, with the support it needs from any and all necessary elements at the client. Those of you who are not consulting to corporations will have less of this to deal with. Corporations are replete with conflicting agendas. You have to be at least a small part of that ecosystem.

---

[1]This term refers to moving the work product from test and development systems to production, where it is really running the business.

Mapping an organization politically is a valuable exercise. The organizational chart is only the beginning! You must map the mentor relationships, connect the internal working relationships, determine what the voting blocs consist of, and bring in the vendor allegiances and other external partnerships.

Sustained and tireless marketing of the project with your client is required to overcome the routine changes in agendas and priorities. As well, for a project of any substance, you do not want to be completely tied to one person at the client. That person may change jobs or even change his or her allegiance to the project. Remember the directive earlier in this chapter to communicate until the client confirms they have had enough? Well, here is one area where that mentality becomes very important. You may even get tired of repeating yourself about the merits of the project. However, you are communicating not to your satisfaction, but to the satisfaction and understanding of the client.

Lest your constant public relations about the project get off the mark, let me remind you of the more salient factors for communication. Your project is solving pain, generating ROI, and otherwise making life more worth living for your clients. Keep the spotlight on their needs, not on yours.

Action Plan

✓ Practice open and honest communication and good listening in all your communications.

✓ When you have a client, over-communicate using the techniques in this chapter.

✓ When you have a client, develop a weekly status report.

✓ When you have a client, schedule weekly status meetings.

Chapter 13

Writing and Speaking

In this chapter I am going to review some of the ways to enhance your image and get the word out about who you are, what your views are, and what you can do for clients. Writing and speaking are intensely interesting skills for consultants to possess, but by no means should these skills be limited to those in consulting.

Writing Articles

Getting your articles into circulation is helpful to a consultant from so many perspectives. One, your name is at the forefront of people's minds in association with your domain. As opportunities for consulting arise, this will help, especially if the article was spot-on to the issue the client is dealing with at the time. However, you cannot expect that every article you get published will lead to direct business. In reality, writing articles is not primarily about direct business. Your articles plant seeds to help future business come more easily.

The second benefit is that writing articles forces you to crystallize your thoughts. Many people know so much about a topic that they can neither condense their understanding into coherent, few-hundred-word bite sizes nor pull out of the topic and discuss the forest as well as the trees. For example, you may know the Oracle database management system inside and out. However, if someone had only a minute to discuss it, could you? How about if someone wanted to discuss its ramifications on the overall business environment? Those who write articles have broached ideas like these and have added knowledge—as well as the organization of that knowledge—to their repertoire.

Third, articles show a dedication to one's craft. Writing articles shows you are serious about your business and your reputation, and you are doing more than what is seemingly immediately necessary.

Publishing helps consulting on many levels.

Fourth, not to be overlooked is that there is a comfort factor in the consultant hiring process for those who are published. A manager can feel comfortable sharing the results of your consultancy, especially strategic deliverables, upwards in his or her organization, knowing that you are credentialed and have some tangible evidence of your authority.

Fifth, you are building a valuable body of documents you can leave behind in hard-copy form or email to your clients and prospects, showing your expertise. I go on few calls now where something does not come up about something I have a published piece on, which makes for a great value-add to a follow-up email.

Finally, you are proving your communications skills and putting them on display. Everybody in almost every business claims good communications skills. These skills are immensely important to your success. And you will have written, published evidence of yours.

Other than any direct and specific benefit you may get from an article, the benefits really accrue after multiple impressions. Don't count on phone calls and emails coming on the heels of each article published.

While some choose to look with disdain at someone who parades his knowledge, the vast majority of people have nothing but respect for it. Don't let the naysayers make you feel uncomfortable with writing articles or otherwise getting yourself out there. It bears repeating: Articles help to justify hiring you and those consultants associated with you, as well as help justify your higher rates. Period.

There are books on writing articles. I do not yet know whether I am good at it. However, I do know that I have hundreds of articles in publication. The first one took me the evenings of an entire week to complete—and I was on vacation in Hawaii while doing it! Now I'm at the point where, once inspiration strikes, I can write an article rather quickly. Sure, sometimes I repeat ideas I've written about before. That is not undesirable. You should stand for something. Just don't repeat the same words—especially if you have surrendered copyright.

NOTE

One example of a book on how to write articles is the aptly titled *Writer's Digest Handbook of Magazine Article Writing* (Writer's Digest, 2004).

> ## CALLING ON ALL SKILLS
>
> You may be saying, "William, I want to be a top consultant, but I have no writing and/or speaking skills. How can I 'just do' these things I am not cut out for?"
>
> Don't sell yourself short on these skills. We have all written. We have all spoken. Give it a try. I had a hard time at first, but try to keep at it to get the hang of it. It is well worth your time. If writing or public speaking just doesn't work for you, you are most likely not going to be Jane Guru or even John Multicapable. That's okay—David Others and Jodi Broker will do quite well in this business, and maybe that's you. If so, you eventually will want to secure someone into your firm who can and will be the public image through writing and speaking.

So, do you write the article first or find the outlet first? You can go either way with this one. The outlet (with commensurate deadline) will help force you to do it. However, writing the article allows you to get it right before you go to market with it. If your article is timely, the latter approach may result in an unwanted delay to its publication.

My experience is that there are a number of print outlets and many more web-based ones for good articles. As long as your article is not a real dud, you will find an outlet for it. Even the higher-circulation and better-regarded magazines (and their websites) will give new authors a shot—usually within rigid bounds in terms of topic, word count, and deadlines. As you expand your portfolio of writing, publishers will be less apt to foist topics upon you, but they still obviously have deadlines and word count guidelines.

I have a monthly column in a major magazine in my industry. It forces me to create at least one article each month. My deadline is the first of each month. The articles are published two months later. My word count limit has changed over the years. It has been in the 800 to 1,000 range. Consultants should commit to writing articles monthly for a periodical. It will be the force that you need to begin building your article base.

Public Speaking

Speaking engagements are excellent venues for direct contact with potential buyers of your services. This is an additional, important benefit of speaking over and above writing. Furthermore, you will get the attention of people who seek their education through attending conferences and talks instead of writing. Otherwise, all six benefits of writing are true for speaking. The historical record of your speaking engagement serves as your "published" record, the equivalent of an article. The impact and benefit of your talk will be felt by many individuals beyond those in the audience.

The two barriers you need to transcend are:

- Getting a speaking engagement
- Engaging an audience when it's time to speak

Speaking isn't over once the engagement is secured.

You are likely working in the industry you will be consulting in, and therefore, you should know what some of the major conferences are. However, even though I have been in some form of information management for my entire career, I still do periodic web searches for new conferences, seminars, breakfast briefings, and the like to see what is going on and where I might propose to speak next.

There are independent organizations that put on vendor-neutral, education-oriented conferences. These are the best outlets for establishing credibility. They are also the most difficult to get established in. The talks there are generally longer—half a day to a full day—and often you have to stay away from touting a particular vendor's goods, which is something many consultants find difficult to do since they have built-up prejudices, and vendors have provided the majority of their education.

There are also the vendor shows, large to small, that put on their user conferences. Unlike the independent shows, at these you must not be vendor neutral. If you are not discussing vendor products, you'll at least need to be focused on a theme that the vendor is currently supporting.

> ### SPEAKING AT PROMOTIONAL EVENTS
> If and when you achieve status in your field, you may also offer your services—either as a fee or just for the exposure—to be the featured speaker at promotional events, where you focus on a trend the vendor is interested in, and the vendor then speaks about their product(s).

Regardless, you should create your hit list of conferences at which you want to speak. Browse the sites looking for calls for papers,[1] communicate your interest to the conference coordinators, and understand the due dates for abstracts and the dates of the conference (so you can hold the date in case you are selected). When you communicate with the coordinators, ask what topics they anticipate to be interested in but short-handed on speakers. Study abstracts from previous conferences to understand the phrasing style that the conference prefers.

Do not be discouraged if you are not selected for a conference. Many times speaking slots are given to conference sponsors. Conference sponsorship is costly and will not be beneficial to a consultant until you have at least a $1 million to $3 million practice. To get around this, you can rightfully play the "I'm just a little guy without a sponsorship budget" card. If they know you have a budget, however, that will be on the table during the consideration of your speaking slot.

Rejection may also occur because:

There are many reasons out of your control why you may not be selected as a speaker.

- The conference already has its dance card full, and the call for papers is not real.
- You are not speaking the lingo of the conference.
- Your session is a "me too" session, and they already have someone covering the topic.
- The topic is not spot-on for the conference.
- The topic (or abstract) was too basic for the level of attendees.
- The topic (or abstract) was too advanced for the level of attendees.
- The abstract was poorly written.
- Your speaking experience was too limited.

---

[1]Often six months prior to the conference itself

> **NOTE**
>
> Do not let rejection or the process necessarily dissuade you. I attended a conference session one time and immediately thereafter went to the conference organizer and said, "I don't know what you're paying him, but I will do a much better job for you on [the same topic]." I got the slot on that topic at their next conference—the first with my consultancy—and did their next 20 or so conferences.

- The abstract sounded like you were going to do a sales pitch.
- You didn't follow all the directions for submission.
- Your topic was interesting…five years ago.

To maintain his or her reputation, a consultant should give three to five public talks per year. If Jane Guru or John Multicapable is your desired consultant profile, you will want more than this. Unlike vying for consulting, which can have long and confusing sales cycles, shopping for speaking venues is not a lot of work. So keep your speaking number up, but make sure your engagements are at quality shows, with reasonable probability of potential buyers present. Speaking at the Rotary Club does not count.

While you can work on an article or on a presentation day and night, unlike writing, speaking comes down to the time you will spend on stage delivering the goods. There you are; nowhere to run. Getting a speaking engagement is obviously necessary, but many first-time speakers let up after getting the engagement and developing the presentation. If the presentation doesn't go off well, you could lose the ability to utilize that outlet for future talks, as well as lose your confidence as a speaker.

Practice, practice, practice your talk until you have it down. If the talking part is 50 minutes, your full-length practice session should take it to about 55 minutes, because when you're live and when you're new to speaking, you will likely forget some things you wanted to say and/or you may speak more quickly than usual. You may be surprised by how slowly time goes by when you're on stage.

Do what it takes to succeed, even if it's something nobody else is doing or thinking about.

For my first-ever conference talk, I arrived the night before and actually went to the room where I would be speaking. It wasn't even set up yet. As a matter of fact, that was happening all around me. I went to approximately where I would be standing and walked through the whole thing, imagining the audience there. The guys setting up got a kick out of it.

Finish the job! Make the talk engaging, interesting, and useful. You will likely give the talk or some form of it over and over if it goes off well.

ESSENTIAL SKILLS FOR SUCCESSFUL SPEAKING DELIVERY

Here are the essential skills for making a successful presentation:

- **Passion.** If the talk is not important to you, why should it be to the audience?
- **Expertise.** Only real expertise allows your confidence to come through; otherwise, you are faking it.
- **Empathy with the audience.** Do they have enough basis to follow your points? Do they need some more grounding, or are they getting bored because they already know what you are saying?
- **Flexibility.** You should have the ability to change your talk in-flight—perhaps just the speed, but perhaps the content.
- **Slides without too few or too many words.** Slides are a backdrop; you are the focus. Slides should underscore what you are saying, but consider the audience perspective and their ability to truly read slides from all seats as well.
- **Relevancy.** Are you telling the audience what they can actually *do* with the information to achieve personal gain?
- **Articulation.** You don't need to use "big words"—that can actually work against you—but your points need to connect in a logical way.

It's okay to have some notes with you on stage. Unless it's a presentation I have down cold, you will find me on stage with a copy of the presentation with notes in front of me. However, never *read* the slides or your notes. Your talk needs to point out the important points on the slide, using different words than the slide shows. It also needs to go into more detail.

Make sure you know much more about the topic than what is on the slides. Most presentations have a Q&A with the audience at the end. If this is going to be true for yours, anticipate the questions and your answers during your preparation.

Some consultants believe they should hold information close to the vest. I have always been one to offer up lots of good information from the stage. Sure, you may find some—especially consultants (that is, people like *you*)—who will pay attention, fully understand what you are saying, and apply or adapt your techniques to their own practice. You are just hoping that a few clients will find the information useful *and* decide you and yours either have more ability or more bandwidth to actually implement the changes you speak of than they do.

Always place a handful of business cards in front of you and encourage an exchange of cards at the end of the talk. Some venues frown on overt marketing. When this is true, limit your self-promotion from the stage and distribute marketing materials only upon request. Stick around at the end of your talk. It's a time to meet and greet the audience, answer more questions, collect cards, and set up times for more discussion.

Other Channels to Fame

The goal of writing and speaking is fame to position your name in front of prospective buyers. There are a number of other channels that have emerged in recent years. With the recession limiting travel budgets, business has really begun to take advantage of webinars. If you are unfamiliar with webinars, it will take very little time on the Internet to become familiar with what this medium entails.

> Though it sounds quirky, getting famous is your goal.

Webinars can consist of a recording of a live presentation, slides being advanced as someone is speaking, or a person talking to the camera without an accompanying slide deck. Currently, the most reasonable webinar vendor with the features you need is GoToWebinar (www.gotowebinar.com). However, before you sign up to record your webinar, be forewarned that having the knowledge and the speaking ability and developing the presentation are about half the battle. Getting eyeballs on your webinar is going to require some promotion. This promotion needs to start with building your (e)mailing list. Just hanging up your shingle on the web in a few places and maybe doing some search engine optimization for a webinar—or a public seminar, for that matter—is not going to be enough to generate interest.

In the first 90 days (and perhaps forever), you will piggyback your talks onto existing conferences only. As you build up your contacts and find needs, you should consider holding breakfast (or lunch) briefings and webinars for your firm.

When you have something to say—and perhaps as a precursor to articles, because of the brevity of blog entries—a blog is a great medium for disseminating ideas. I encourage you to start one.[2] Blogs must be kept up to date, updated no less frequently than every two weeks, and not be bald-faced sales pitches. Although both articles and blogs are for organizing information, establishing credibility, and generating leads, there are separate reasons for articles and blogs. Blogs do achieve all six of the benefits discussed earlier, although usually in a somewhat muted fashion— more quantity, less quality.

Blogs are often written in a more personable style, conveying both information and personality to the reader.

NOTE

Please remember that anything on the Internet can be part of your *permanent* record. As time goes on, there is going to be increased access to archival information that you thought you deleted (for example, see www.archive.org). Do not say anything you would not want prospects, clients, vendors, your neighbor, your mother, your spouse, your former boss, your enemies, potential stalkers, and so on to read. Do not blog when you're upset, and never be disrespectful.

Excellent blogs to review for ideas include:

- Those at www.b-eye-network.com (including mine)
- Circaspecting at circaspecting.typepad.com/ circaspecting_musings_on_
- Datadoodle at www.datadoodle.com
- Jonathan Schwartz's blog at blogs.sun.com/jonathan

The dilemma comes in where you are going to host your blog. You can certainly put it on your website. However, be realistic

---

[2]But, please, it's "when you have something to say"—if you're not sure, do three to four entries and stage them to the blog over time.

about the investment you are making in SEO and in updating content to drive traffic to your site. As with public speaking, hanging up your shingle (in this case, your blog) is not enough. That's why it may make sense to join a site that has a consortium of blogs and promotes them heavily—because site hits drive their revenue. You may have to share the site with blogs closely competitive to yours, but you don't find Subway restaurants in the middle of the desert. They're usually located within steps of other eats, with everyone benefitting from the traffic.

If you can't find one of these that will take on your blog, and you don't want to host your blog on your site, you can start a blog today at sites such as IT.toolbox.com, blogspot.com, and typepad.com. You can link to them from your site. Try to get a site (TypePad is particularly good) that doesn't decorate the perimeter with too many annoying advertisements.

Whatever way you go, make sure your blog entries are promoted appropriately (coded with the keywords you want to be known for) to the following: Technorati, Digg, Furl, and Delicious. If you don't know what those are, getting familiar is as easy as browsing the sites. New social tagging and bookmarking sites are popping up weekly as I write this. As with the Twitter ranking and so on, *anything* you try that is working for you—*keep it up*! Although I would not recommend investing too much time in trying to get top spots on any of these, if your interest and proclivities lie along these lines (and they should if your consulting has anything to do with social networking), go for it. Consulting business models can be built on this.

> Go with what is working for you. There are many outlets.

> **NOTE**
> Hopefully, you can appreciate the mixed messages throughout this book. Consulting is not linear, and there is no one size fits all.

There are also numerous other venues for your content, seemingly only limited by the collective imagination of the web-savvy new media world. These include unsponsored white papers, podcasts, tips, and so on. These aren't necessarily "first 90 days" outlets for you, but keep them on your radar.

I discussed some social media in Chapter 5 in terms of using it for staying current in your field. However, social media is interactive. You get to contribute. The point of mentioning it here when talking about fame is that I do not currently consider Twitter, Facebook, MySpace, Yelp, Blip.fm, SlideShare, and all of their cousin sites on the Internet to be particularly effective today at helping with the goals of this chapter—outlets for content to make yourself known in your field. Where they *can* be effective is in link-baiting[3] to your good stuff. However, for link-baiting to work, you need to give to as well as take from the medium, so we are back to the dilemma regarding effective use of your time.

Weeding Through the Feedback

In terms of quantity of inquiries, your fame will certainly turn up more noise than real, live prospects. And I don't mean the people who are in your target audience who don't have any budget at the moment for your services. Those are prospects. Answer their questions. I also don't mean inquisitive technicians who, in their current position, are in no position to hire consultants. They may go places; you never know. Those are prospects. Answer their questions as best and as nicely as you can without spending too much time on them. Those are prospects—albeit future prospects—and furthermore, it's hopefully rewarding and intellectually productive to answer good questions and establish community.

The noise I speak of comes in the form of inquires such as:

- Would you write an article for our magazine? (This is usually of much lesser value to you than the one you just wrote for.)

- Would you speak at our event? (This is usually of much lesser value to you than the one you just spoke at.)

- I'm a college student, and I'm writing a paper...

- I need some career advice...

- I would like to show you our product... (Maybe you do, maybe you don't.)

It's your call on these. Use your judgment. It may be opportunity knocking, or it may be the consultant equivalent of junk mail.

---

[3]Posting links to your content

Action Plan

✓ Write your first article.

✓ List the publications in which you want to get published and contact them about submitting articles and/or taking on a column.

✓ Create your target list of public speaking forums and their upcoming calls for papers.

✓ Undoubtedly, there will be some open calls, so develop abstract(s) and submit.

✓ Find a blog outlet and start a blog.

PART III

Beyond Initial Success

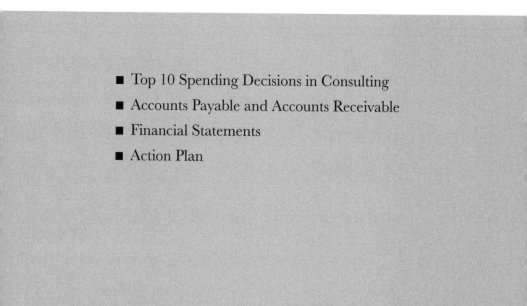

Chapter 14

Managing Capital

- Top 10 Spending Decisions in Consulting
- Accounts Payable and Accounts Receivable
- Financial Statements
- Action Plan

I have continually emphasized the gross revenue[1] aspect of the consulting bottom line, and I believe that is where the emphasis needs to be. We spend most of our time and energy on the revenue side of the ledger. If you run a conservative business, the revenue less the direct expenses of contractor pay rates and employee (fully burdened) salaries can be primarily considered the bottom line. However, that's a big *if*. I will caution you in the final chapter about discretionary personal spending, but what about discretionary business spending? What is discretionary?

Here, once again, we have to bring our best friend, personal judgment, into the action. In a general sense, you should be aware of what degree you are presently expanding the business. In tight times, which are often the right times to invest and establish a foothold in a market that is going to open up with better days, some firms go into "keep the lights on" mode. This can be a very difficult situation for all involved—management, employees, and even vendors and clients. Managing through tough times as well as good times can be challenging.

In this chapter, I will address the top 10 spending decision points that you will need to make related to money. Many of these are addressed in detail elsewhere in the book, but seeing them all here together, listed as the major spending decision points, can give you some context. If you've been reading along and deciding to spend on everything I've mentioned, then thinking about all the spending together, which is what you need to do, could obviate that strategy.

I recommend a conservative approach to spending whereby every major purchase (say, greater than $2,000) is put against two vital tests, which are:

- How much more consulting will I need to sell to pay for this?[2]
- How will this help me sell that consulting?

I prefer this approach as opposed to just budgeting an amount for marketing and spending that down. It will help you keep a tighter rein on your bottom line. There is no doubt that some ongoing spend is required for the business, though.

---

[1]Revenue minus direct expenses of the delivery, such as contractor or employee costs

[2]Translate average gross margin into revenue, so if average gross margin is 33 percent, you would need to sell $6,000 more in consulting to pay for a $2,000 investment.

Top 10 Spending Decisions in Consulting

Let's look at some guidelines for the top 10 spending decisions you'll need to make. Keep in mind that these will apply to your consulting to varying degrees depending on your concept. If you are an employee at a consultancy, these either are determined for you or at least are joint decisions with the consultancy founders.

1. Hire or Contract the Billable Team

Let's start with the biggest issue. This one is even *pre*–gross margin! Hiring is a growth mode activity, which hopefully you believe you are in. It also gives you the most flexibility around assignments and gives clients comfort with the close, seemingly longer-term arrangements you have with the consultants. You can manage the domains the employees grow in per the vision and outlook for the company. On the downside, there are the potential gaps in billing, which loom even larger when the individual is not helpful in sales cycles. Employees also rightfully expect more caretaking from the firm. Contracting is obviously safer. Once the billing is done, so is your commitment. Then, there are the gray areas between the two extremes. Your people are strategic to the business. You should accumulate strength in the firm. More in Chapter 10, "Acquiring People," on this important decision point.

2. Hire Sales

Hiring sales is really tough to justify for a small firm—until *you* establish the concept and get it to a reasonable level, say, of running $500,000 annual income. The founder is usually the lead salesperson! Those with ambition in consulting who say they "don't do sales" are in for a rough road. Your personal time, your biggest asset, may get split across sales and delivery. Chapter 1 talked about the different profiles. You may actually change profiles over time and change how much you spend on one versus the other. Most founders and practice leaders (except the gurus) are going to find their sales skills are the necessary skills for elevating the company, even more so than the delivery—unless the delivery is unusually complex.

A salesperson is not a salesperson is not a salesperson. A consultant is not a consultant is not a consultant. It's better to be opportunistic about the best talent available than to scramble to fit an urgent need. If a talented salesperson or consultant comes into your path who appears to be a fit, look for a way to make it happen rather than always making last-minute hires.

3. Pay for or Self-Build Marketing

If it's your domain (in other words, you're a marketing consultant) or you happen to be particularly competent at something or have the proclivity to get competent quickly, do it for yourself. Otherwise, selectively utilize outside services to complete these items, especially if you can trust the quality of the service due to a relationship, referral, and so on.

Back in Chapter 3, when I talked about needing a website, I provided some of the parameters around paying someone to build one for you or building one yourself, based on skills and quality needed. I'll reiterate here that the main point is upkeep. You don't want to pay for upkeep and changes with your money or in lag time.

As for other marketing materials I spoke of in Chapter 3, there again you can go inexpensive to high-quality and expensive. The control factor (over changing content, printing on demand, distribution, and so on) is more important than anything else. If your marketing material is going to be changing frequently, and clients will be understanding about this and accepting of a lower standard of quality, you can do those pieces yourself. High-fee, specialized, static consulting offerings may demand more professionalism, and therefore, you would pay for those pieces to be done professionally.

4. Have a Board

If you want expert advisement for your particular firm, you can find it. If you have to go beyond friends and family, you must be prepared to give up something. It may be some money, but more likely you are looking to *quid pro quo* the situation (which is a two-way street) or perhaps offer some level of ownership (discussed in Chapter 15, "Partnerships"). You may catch the eye of someone who can provide advisement without anything overt in return, but don't count on it and don't disappoint their expectations, which may be that they will get a piece if it ever becomes worth anything. I have always been able to *quid pro quo* my outside advisement and have found very formal boards and any associated expenses to not be worth it—but to each his own.

5. Office Space

Don't neglect creating corporate culture just because you don't have an office. Weekly meetings, perhaps using Live Meeting, GoToMeeting, or just a conference call, are good for communication within the company.

This can really dig into the bottom line early on. If you decide to use an outside office, your profile of low-cost/non-swanky to high-cost/swanky will be determined by your need to see clients in that office. Most concepts will not need too much of this because most consulting is done at client sites. As you grow, at about the $750,000 annual revenue level, when you have several consultant employees with bench time or doing client activities offsite, it makes sense to have a centrally located office.

6. Annual Bonuses

If you have followed the advice of Chapter 10 and have established some flexibility around the pay profiles of your employees, when the firm has a good year, it is a good idea to unexpectedly share some annual bonuses with key employees. There should be a rhyme and reason to the amounts. You do not want the employees to get into a game of deciphering who got the most. Don't expect employees to come to the rationalization that, "Well, this annual bonus is just part of my overall package, which includes base, performance, and utilization bonus, and John over there may have got a higher annual bonus, but his overall pay package probably leaves him somewhat underpaid, so it's understandable that he received a higher annual bonus than I."

7. Accounting and Legal

Finally, I get to assert something as a definite spend. Accounting, in the sense of your annual taxes (federal and state), advisement on quarterly estimates to pay (federal and state), what you can expense to the business, and so on is an ongoing part of the business. Tax laws are inevitably changing and not getting any less complex. For a business of any size, I recommend outside accounting. It's their job to keep up with the tax law changes, think about creative ways to reduce tax burdens for small businesses, and efficiently deliver the requirements to the government.

Legal advisement is going to be feast or famine. You will want to have legal advisement on speed dial, but hopefully you will seldom need it. I recommend tossing your attorney a bone every now and then to keep the relationship open and to allow you to ask the simple questions that crop up without feeling like you are out of line.

Taxes and IRS fees are a big expense as well, but since you don't have much flexibility there, they're not included in this list! Personally, when it comes to small bills, I just keep a number in my head, and if it's below that, it gets paid without any thought[3]. It's more effort than it's worth to track it down.

8. Bookkeeping, Accounts Payable/Accounts Receivable

If you can find a quality resource who will be time and materials at whatever scale you need or who will give you a small block of time (say, four hours per week) to cover bookkeeping, accounts payable, and accounts receivable (and, while we're at it, other things you may need from an assistant!), it is well worth it.

Can a qualified spouse or other family member do the functions of bookkeeping and assistant? It is more harmful in the long run (to both business and family) to hire unqualified and inappropriate family members.

---

[3]It is said that Albert Einstein wore the same thing every day to save himself from wasting brain energy on fashion.

Keep in mind that bookkeeping is different from accounting. Whereas the accountant is critical up front and on a periodic basis, you will have much more triage with the bookkeeper.

9. Conference and Training Attendance and Sponsorship

If you've been accepted to speak at a conference (refer to Chapter 13), your conference attendance is complimentary. Hopefully, you picked strategic conferences to submit to in the first place, so this one's a no-brainer. Pay for the travel and go. Attendance otherwise should be subject to the following criteria. Will the attendance allow you to:

- Keep up with the latest technology, methods, lingo, and so on?
- Find out what your competition is doing?
- Meet prospective clients and find out what they are talking about?
- Network with professionals in your field to stay in the front of their minds?
- Deepen relationships with professionals and clients?

This all goes for your employees as well. They have the same needs, and you have the education obligation.

The same criteria should be applied to the countless ways that conference organizers make sponsorships available. If the criteria are measurably heightened by sponsorship, it may be time to sponsor—although this tends to make sense in a more developed company, and not as a first-90-days activity.

10. Technology Environment

Love of technology is not lost on consultants, many of whom utilize technology either directly or indirectly in their work with clients. Some will want to funnel some money into having a technical lab of sorts in order to test new technology, understand the latest releases, and perhaps do some real client work. This can get into big money when compared to your revenue stream, and there are some less expensive measures that can be utilized to accomplish the same objectives.

Much software—even enterprise software—works on personal computers. It may not have all the same features and functions as software that needs UNIX, but that may be acceptable for your testing and development needs. There are also virtual machine images that allow you to be on anyone else's computer and have access to their resources. And there are lower-cost alternatives to enterprise-class machines, such as the open-source Linix operating system and associated software.

In general, I recommend utilizing these lower-cost approaches. However, you (should) know your business best. If having the additional technology opens up doors for a new offering that will provide the practice with return on investment, do it. Make it pay for itself. If there are tangential benefits to the technology, then consider it a bonus.

Now you can see that there are no mystery expenses to consulting. I've sprinkled them throughout the book. Keep them in check and in line with your bottom-line objectives. Now, let's discuss paying them…and getting paid ourselves!

Asking whether business skills are important to your consultancy is a bit like asking whether a professional basketball player needs to be able to shoot the ball well. You can get away with little shooting ability, but you won't make it unless you are unbelievable at rebounding and defense. If you lack business skills, you will have to make up for it with other strengths.

Accounts Payable and Accounts Receivable

As far as the logistics around paying these expenses, you will want to bulk them up and not think about them continually. Unless you are hiring employees and contractors who live from paycheck to paycheck, once a month should be sufficient for those accounts payables for a small consultancy. The same goes for the ongoing expenses: phone(s), website, subscriptions, office or post office/PMB box, outside services, business charge card, and so on.

Organize this area of your practice using what your bookkeeper and accountant need to do their jobs. Keep personal items separate from those for the business.

Likewise, unless you are particularly concerned about the risk of not getting paid by a client, structuring their payments monthly should be fine. When I spoke of contracts in Chapter 9, I talked about this variable. Unfortunately, accounts receivable is a process and not as automatic as it may seem. Clients may have different standards as to how they are billed. Invoices may need a number, may need to go to a remote location, may need to be accompanied by client-approved timesheets, and so on. It's a hassle.

And then there's the follow-through on getting payments if they become late. It is good if you can get your bookkeeper to perform this function. However, judge appropriately. If your only contact at the client is one (or a few) people, which doesn't include anybody particularly connected to the payment process, they may not be open to having a separate relationship with your bookkeeper nagging them about payments. Rest assured, you must be paid. You are in a value-for-value relationship, and payment is a big part of the value you realize from the relationship. However, the manner in which you go about asserting this right is part of your overall relationship and should be handled with care.

Look at almost any attorney's bill. It's detailed and fairly bulletproof to challenge. This is a good model for your invoices.

Whether it's per-hour or fixed consulting that you and yours are engaged in, keeping track of what will need to be billed at month end is essential to do *daily*. Busy people can easily forget how many hours they worked for a client yesterday. Ensure ledgering by yourself and each consultant on a daily basis for billable events, such as hours worked on a time-and-materials engagement, fixed-fee consulting delivered, and travel expenses incurred that will be reimbursed. It is also a good idea (again daily) to notate a sentence or two for each client about *what* was done. This can come in handy should any billing be challenged. Remember the ethical nature of recording hours as discussed in Chapter 7.

NOT GETTING PAID BY THE CLIENT

I suppose I am lucky because I have never been stiffed by a client. However, a few times I have dealt with a multi-month, prolonged payment cycle due to client business challenges or unspoken late requirements about the process of payment. And I've had colleagues who have had to write off substantial amounts ($40,000 to $150,000). Honestly, I can't even fault them for it in all cases. The clients went under (in which case you just get in line) or challenged the work product. I'm in no place to judge the merits of those work products that were challenged, but the contract language (as interpreted by the legal system) will ultimately rule. Use your judgment, but you may well need to assert your rights through the legal system. If you follow the advice of Chapter 9 about contracts, you should be pretty well protected.

Despite contract language, clients whose business is teetering on its last legs are risky clients on which to bank your business. You should seek shorter, maybe weekly, payment cycles and immediately raise a flag if a payment is ever late.

Do not allow the client to distract you from seeking payments you are due. Often, the people you deal with have not run businesses and don't understand that timely payments are critical to a small business or a consulting practice. The accounts payable department may be several layers of the organization away from them, and they may be disinterested in the laborious chore of navigating the organization to help get you paid. Be assertive about payment on Day 2 of lateness. After two to three weeks of no progress, you need to be willing to pull back the work effort and take it to another level.

Unfortunately, the first other level that is prudent is going to be a collections agency, which will pursue the claim for you without your elegance and ineffectiveness, for 25 to 50 percent take. The good news is there's seldom an upfront fee to collections. After a month of this, it's time to see whether both parties can agree to mediation, in which case an independent arbiter (not an attorney or judge) listens to both sides and renders a binding decision. If the client won't agree to mediation (or for some reason you won't), take them to court. You will likely be above the small claims thresholds here, but your attorney will help you seek interest, damages, business lost, and so on.

Is this all ugly and drawn out? Yes, but you may need to exercise the process. Don't stand on principle, however. Settle for 60 to 75 percent, lick your wounds, and move on if you can. The process needs to be exercised when communication has broken off.

I deal with new international clients. Imagine going to Malaysia—a 24-hour trip for me—to do work for a client you have never met and cannot gauge the reputation of, all for the promise of a net 30 payment, which will take place when you're 3,000 miles away, back at home. I'm not going to do that, and neither should you. In this case, I need some large measure of the payment upfront—in the bank account and cleared—before I will commit my time allocation and my funds to booking the flight. I may also need to apply this level of diligence to a client just across town if they are a big red flag—that is, in bankruptcy, in the news for all the wrong reasons, or risky based on what I know or otherwise intuit about them.

On balance, despite these admonitions, not getting paid is not a problem in consulting if you exercise good judgment.

In addition to accounts receivable, you also need to keep track of upcoming accounts payables. Knowing *when* you will need money is important in your overall business financial plan.

Financial Statements

Operate your business on a cash basis, not an accrual basis, which recognizes revenue at the time it is earned instead of collected. You may have a few months in the beginning where the books do not look well, but in the long run, the lesser amount of paperwork will pay off.

If you are organized with your finances, you are a few short steps away from the financial statements that are required. First, you will need an income statement (see Figure 14.1). An income statement shows the income, expenses, and net earnings (or loss) for a specified period of time. Second, you will need a balance sheet, as shown in Figure 14.2. A balance sheet provides a point-in-time look at the firm's assets (that is, bank accounts, equipment, accounts receivable), liabilities (in other words, accounts payable), and equity, which is the difference between the two.

If you are employed at a consultancy, there may be a standard format for these for your practice, or they may be developed by the accounting team for you.

Figure 14.1

Sample income statement.

REVENUE:		
Services	$	394,000
Other		17,000
		411,000
COST OF REVENUE:		
Services		245,000
Consultant expenses		25,000
		270,000
GROSS PROFIT		141,000
OPERATING EXPENSES		
Selling and marketing		24,000
General and administrative		18,000
Depreciation and amortization		4,000
		46,000
PROFIT BEFORE INCOME TAXES		95,000
INCOME TAXES		-12,000
NET INCOME		83,000

ASSETS		
CURRENT ASSETS		
Cash	$	22,000
Accounts receivable, net		37,000
Prepaid expenses		5,000
TOTAL CURRENT ASSETS		64,000
PROPERTY AND EQUIPMENT, at cost, net		25,000
Other assets		13,000
Total Assets		102,000
LIABILITIES		
CURRENT LIABILITIES		
Accounts payable and accrued expenses		33,000
TOTAL CURRENT LIABILITIES		
Owner's Equity		69,000
Total Liabilities and Owner's Equity		102,000

Figure 14.2
Sample balance sheet.

If you do not do the statements monthly, at least do them quarterly. A third report is the statement of changes in financial position, which shows changes in account values over time and the corresponding reasons why. This can be helpful in seeing changes in the finances of the business, but realistically, small-business owners should know intuitively how the firm is doing financially. These reports will be essential if you ever get close to your exit strategy, discussed in Chapter 17, "Marketable Value and Exit Strategies."

Keep in mind that your salary is part of the cost of revenue.

Whatever the statements and your intuition show about the business, I don't believe it factors much into your activities on the sales side of the business. Your objective remains the same in good times and in bad times—sell as much as possible when you are able to deliver the client superior value. Forecasting is almost a black art in consulting, but if it is a motivating factor, go for it.

CURRENT AND LONG-TERM

Both assets and liabilities are further segmented into current and long-term. Current assets include cash and other assets that can be easily converted to cash within a year. Likewise, current liabilities are debts that will be paid within a year. Long-term assets and liabilities are expected to be on the books after a year.

Action Plan

✓ Set up a system for logging billable activities until it's time for billing.

✓ Hire a bookkeeper, or get to know your accounting group if you are employed at a consultancy.

✓ Set up a system for tracking your hours and fees to bill.

✓ Set up a system for paying bills.

✓ With your accountant and bookkeeper, create a system for tracking expendable items and doing the financial reports.

Chapter 15

Partnerships

- Oh, the People You'll Meet in Consulting
- Partnership Business Formation
- Deal-Based Partnerships
- Partnerships with Vendors
- Action Plan

I will focus on two kinds of partnerships in this chapter. The first is the business formation that is a partnership. The second is partnerships with vendors. Both come down to relationships with people, so there will be an initial focus on getting along with others in consulting. There are softer factors in dealing with any other person, and while Chapter 8 dealt with client relationships and Chapter 10 with acquiring people, the softer factors in those and all relationships, including with your business and vendor partners, are critical to relationship success.

Homo sapiens have prospered as a species due to their unique ability to cooperate for mutual gain. We find partnerships of various kinds throughout our business world. This is especially true in America, where dozens of business entities gain or lose when another does the same. You can greatly compound your contribution to your primary responsibilities—your clients and your consultancy—with good partnerships.

Oh, the People You'll Meet in Consulting

People in consulting you'll interact with include clients, their management, their subordinates, their consultants, other consultants, your consultants, vendors, sales, marketing, public relations, lawyers, accountants, employees, and so on.

To establish a partnership of any sort or to really get much done in consulting, you need to enjoy and give value to people from all walks of life, holding various amounts of authority over you and bringing all manner of ideas—founded and unfounded—to the table. Tactfulness in these interactions goes beyond following formulas. However, I believe I can share some skills you can develop and be cognizant of that will improve your ability to succeed with the people in consulting.

Consulting relationships can be much more temporal than those you had in the employee world. In the employee world, while surely there is change in the players around you, often you will see and interact with Joe, Jane, and Sue every day. While Jane may have irritated you when you first met, you have learned to live with her quirks (and she with yours, hopefully) over time. However, a new Jane doesn't necessarily come into your life every week or every day. In consulting, there are new Janes very frequently. The good and bad news is that the duration of the relationships, even the good ones, tends to be either short or with intermittent contact only. This is not to say you will not have long-term relationships. You will—especially if you take on partners. However, you will most definitely also have short, intermittent relationships, and this is where your practice can excel or fail.

The three characteristics that are essential in your consulting relationships are professionalism, low ego, and respect. Obviously, these work together. Take away any one, and it's like a house of cards in the relationship. You cannot respect others when your ego is getting in the way. Nor is it professional to not show respect for others.

It means genuinely caring for the other person's interest in the relationship. It means not finishing their sentences or talking over them. Yet, at the same time, you respect their time enough to be ready with your responses and not keep them waiting. You are looking for the win-win in the interaction.

You actually do need to be ready to speak when the other person is finished. Pregnant pauses show that you are listening, but even they should come naturally.

Differences of opinion on various matters are normal. Resolving them amicably requires effort on your part. It would be great if everybody subscribed to professionalism, low ego, and respect at this point. You can't control whether other people do, but you always should. At a tactical level, if someone talks over you, you shouldn't act upset and start doing it too. You can decide after the interaction whether this is someone you want to work with, but stay in the game by always being professional and showing respect.

I previously talked about the balance, or imbalance, that clients show in wanting to get tasks done quickly, then adding features and functions, and back again. While in a client deliverable situation, you will find some of this Jekyll-Hyde syndrome—usually people tend to behave in one of a few ways. It is important to understand the modus operandi that the person you are dealing with is coming from.

- Get it over with
- Get it perfect
- Makest thou me no waves
- A healthy combination

Getting it over with means, "Get this interaction over with as soon as possible so I can do other, more important things![1] Get to the point. Spare me the details!" Your mission is set in this interaction. Get to the point. Spare her the details and get out. If there are items that you absolutely need to address that she is unaware of, they may need to wait until another time. Or, if you must

---

[1]Or do nothing; some people are just programmed to force conversations to the point.

address them, do so showing complete respect for her time, perhaps prefacing it with, "This will only take a minute," and/or "This is important, or I wouldn't take another minute of your time for it."

You find the "get it perfect" school of thought a lot with IT professionals. Hey, you just do. Perhaps they subscribe to a book standard on how things need to be done, or maybe they have become creatures of habit over the years of doing their work and projecting some unnecessary rigor or steps into a process. It could also be that they're the ones who are going to have to live with your work after you're gone, and they fear calls in the middle of the night to address failures. In this case, your mission is to make sure you acknowledge and address their quality concerns.

The "makest thou me no waves" people show a lot of deference to you in the relationship because they are just too nice to challenge and/or do not want to hold responsibility for the outcome. Although this may seem like a prime situation to just go and take what you want, this can be as challenging a situation as any because you need to extract their opinion in order to ultimately get their sustainable buy-in.

A healthy combination is best if you have it or can develop it. It is also best for your potential partners. I have to stress these "getting along" characteristics of any partnership as first and foremost in making it work. People generally getting along and accepting one another can tend to work things out, whereas partnerships between people without the ability to do that are doomed to fail.

Partnership Business Formation

I have often observed that many of the truly successful consultancies are partnerships. However, these are not simply partnerships of convenience or random collections of dissatisfied ex-corporatists. These are truly partnerships where all partners take a "separate but equal" approach to the business. These are partnerships where all the tasks to be done are covered by one or more of the partners, both from a skill and from a desire perspective. These are partnerships where partners give equal and high effort toward the goals. These are partnerships where the partners portray a healthy combination of the various perspectives mentioned earlier in their communications with other partners.

If something works, you need to decide whether you're going to challenge it. Retraining others in another way may end up taking more time than just letting things go. Of course, you should not allow self-destructive behavior, and your client may or may not be expecting you to exercise control over the process.

By keeping ears, eyes, and mind open, you will know where others are coming from and can react appropriately with low ego, professionalism, and respect.

Equal-ownership partnerships are the only practical way to divide ownership. This would be 50-50 for two people, 33-33-33 for three people, and so on.

However, many more have failed and/or resulted in the bitter loss of friendships than have succeeded. You *must* get into the partnership, as with a marriage,[2] with a firm understanding of roles, responsibilities, and benefits. Each partner is accountable to every other partner. And, most importantly—because it's overlooked and somewhat messy—you need an agreement as to how partners get *out* and new partners get *in*, as well as how the partnership triggers an exit strategy.[3]

All marriages may not have prenuptial agreements, but all business partnerships should.

PARTNERSHIP "LIGHT"

There are partnerships of convenience, whereby the partnership is formed simply to spare each otherwise independent consultant the personal cost of business insurance, a website and some other marketing, and so on. In these, ultimately everybody "eats what they kill." These are beneficial, and I'm not against them. Just don't get into a business formation of a partnership for these things thinking that it's simple. Even the website could create disagreements! Talk. Document. Up front! Be prepared to walk away if it's not a fit.

Here are some of the main areas where partners need to agree:

- Services to be offered
- Spending levels by category
- Branding
- Titles
- Prospect tracking and sharing
- Bringing in others—partners, employees, contractors, and so on
- Seed money
- Website design and update strategy
- Marketing materials
- Business insurance
- Separate, or single, profit and loss statements and strategies
- Revenue sharing

---

[2]Or a band—see the movie *Anvil: The Story of Anvil* for a look at a lasting partnership.
[3]Exit strategies will be discussed in Chapter 17, "Marketable Value and Exit Strategies."

- Contribution of one to the other's business development
- Benefits
- Employee bench strategy
- Events
- Newsletter
- Vendor partnerships
- Recruiting
- Roles and responsibilities
  - Website
  - Administration
  - Accounting
  - Insurance
  - Benefits
  - Newsletter
  - Vendor partnerships
- Salaries and how they may be adjusted
- Exit strategy

Be sure to utilize an attorney in preparing the partnership documents.

Some measure of a financial partnership is recommended to help make that 1+1=3 and guarantee interest by all parties in all firm business. There are various parts to each dollar of gross profit the company receives. Each dollar could be allocated to the partners in any number of ways. There are the parties who sold the deal, the parties who influenced the deal, the parties who will oversee the deal, and the parties who bill on the deal.[4] And then, finally, there is the partner group. The partner group should be incented on every deal. This is the foundation of the partnership. It's not every man for himself. It's "if you do well, I do well," while still recognizing the direct contributions of each party to each specific deal.

All-out partnerships that do not specifically incent partners to win business but could allow a partner to ride the success of everyone else are not a good idea for partnership setup. There needs to be a balance.

---

[4]If you have a figurehead person for the firm, he or she may be entitled to a piece of every deal, based on the assumption that, even without direct contribution, that person helps bring the business in by being associated with the firm.

The aforementioned formation makes sense if each partner is more or less trying to win business. If a partner is not equal in this sense of contribution to the firm, such as a chief financial officer (CFO) type, then that partner may receive a bigger part of each deal than the others.

For example, the gross profit of a deal can be allocated between two partners anywhere from 90/10 to 50/50, depending on the level of contribution of each across the four components. If one partner did it all with no direct help from the other, it could be split 90/10. It could go to 50/50 if everything was equal. Of course, saying who sold the deal can be subject to interpretation. It helps to be flexible and include multiple people in any of the categories. It also helps to have a general partner type who can ultimately make the allocations if the interested parties disagree—and people who will accept the decisions (which goes back to the "getting along" discussion).

Whew! That's income—the good stuff. Overhead expenses, such as the website, admin (maybe), accounting, insurance, healthcare, 401K, and so on, are usually allocated equally. However, what about allocating those expenses that do not fit overhead or direct to a client exactly? You would not put everyone on the hook 100 percent for expenses they incur in pursuing business, attending conferences, and so on.

And while contractors only incur expenses against billing, what about employee bench time? Does one partner "sponsor" that employee and take the hit on her gross profit/pay calculations, or is the expense allocated equally or 90/10?

> There is more than one way to skin a cat, and there is more than one way to split earnings amongst partners.

> It's very important to accept the terms of the partnership as you enter the partnership. You should not enter a partnership if you resent any part of the agreement or the manner in which the agreement came to be. You should also know your partners and know that they (and probably you) will not change once you're partners.

Deal-Based Partnerships

There are also partnerships in the sense of the word that are formed around specific deals. These partnerships can be established with employees, contractors, outside sales agents, your mother, and so on—whoever might bring in business. We'll call those people, in this role, agents. You want to create a tangible benefit to people for doing that, especially those who may extend your eyes and ears into the market and learn of business that makes sense for the firm. These usually would not affect firm equity distribution, only the gross profit division.

> Money talks. The rest walks. Incent tangibly.

Be careful and specific in any agreements around a definition of gross profit. Since client billing can be either hourly or fixed, and employees or outside consultants can be used in the delivery, it can get a little messy. Defining employee cost is tricky as well. You can't simply take salary divided by 52 (weeks/year) divided by 40 (hours/week). Full employee cost is called *burden cost*. A fully burdened employee cost takes into consideration the cost of her benefits. Depending on the extent of your benefits, this can be anywhere from 15 to 35 percent on top of her salary. And finally, reimbursed travel expenses are no problem, but what if the client isn't picking up the travel?

If you actually carry a profit and loss statement for the client, it gives you the opportunity to put your other expenses into the equation. However, rather than nickel and diming the referring agent, come up with a percentage of the gross profit you can live with that fits a simple definition.

There are four types of gross profit:

- Hourly with outside consultant: Bill rate − (charge rate + unreimbursed travel)

- Hourly with employee: Bill rate − (burden rate × hours + unreimbursed travel and downtime)

- Fixed with outside consultant: Fixed price − cost (in other words, hours × charge rate + unreimbursed travel)

- Fixed with employees: Fixed price − (burden rate × hours + unreimbursed travel and downtime)

For example, you might extend an offer of 20 percent of burdened profit for employee/consultant billings to clients that the agent sells. The percentage may be prorated based on the level of your firm's assistance needed in selling the business. If they just bring the opportunity and you work it to completion, you may find that to be worth 10 percent. If they bring a closed deal, 20 percent.

It is simpler just to calculate the fee based on revenue. However, with a little more work, you can ensure the more important measure of gross profit.

You should put a rider into all these contracts that all deals are subject to verification by you and must be profitable to the firm.

> **NOTE**
> Keep in mind that if you are paying someone as an employee, if you simply pass him all of his billing rate, you are losing money, even if he does not partake of benefits. About the most you can afford is 90 percent of personal billings until billings reach $100,000 in a calendar year. Then, Social Security is paid, and you can go to 98 percent. (To be precise, see where the Social Security limit is set for the year.)

Partnerships with Vendors

It is difficult to significantly innovate in a boutique consultancy, which is generally formed for cash flow. Using technology consulting as an example, usually the innovation is around supporting domains and industries with solutions that are increasingly relevant but utilize software developed by the likes of Microsoft, IBM, Symantec, SAP, HP, EMC, and Cisco, as well as smaller players in your chosen industry and perhaps even open-source software. Partnerships can be developed with these interesting vendors for several reasons and at several levels.

Many vendor partnerships are symbolic. You want logos. They want logos. It's a logo swap under the pretense that you will bring each other business. Some are more serious and actually do result in business. Some (many!) firms are built around a given vendor or vendor offerings.

In these relationships, it is you, the smaller player in the relationship, who often feels like you are giving more than you are receiving. You need to hire or train in the vendor's offerings, try to sell their wares, and so on in order to get their attention and referrals.

> **NOTE**
> Some vendors are more suspicious than others about your firm having partnerships with, or even acknowledging, their competitors. This is a fine line you will need to learn to walk. You often make the "deal with the devil," where you toss aside all pretense of vendor neutrality and any strategic positioning you might have with the market in exchange for the goodies that come with a single vendor partnership.

Not all vendors act with integrity. Even if you bring them a client on a silver platter, they can try to turn the professional services over to their preferred professional services, which is often the PS branch of the vendor company.

Clients who buy from a vendor take the vendor's recommendation for the professional services (PS) part that accompanies the purchase very seriously. Many take it without questioning. That is the Holy Grail you are trying to attain in a serious partnership. You can take it further by doing marketing activities related to the vendor products. Believe me—serious partnerships take work and often require a dedicated partner or senior member of the firm to nurture the relationship.

Many partners with serious vendor relationships also resell the vendor products. In many ways, this is a different beast from selling consulting services, so I will not give it its due in this book. This does take you down the path of being single-vendor aligned as opposed to neutral, which some clients will view as less than positive. Some vendors allow resale only to smaller-end clients for whom they do not staff a sales force, while others allow selling to all profiles of end clients. Follow the money. Many vendor salespeople get the same commission whether you sell it or they sell it. Others are set up in competition with you, and you are less likely to find cooperation with those salespeople.

Want to build the relationship with a vendor? Bring them a deal.

If you are able to create reusable tools, that is great. The margins on software are much higher than consulting. And furthermore, despite recent advances in simulation, I don't believe software will talk back to you or ask for more money, less travel, and more interesting assignments. Software does, however, require upgrades, maintenance, support, and a very supportive infrastructure. Obviously, I won't get into running a software company in this book. However, you should be very aware of this avenue. Again, with our definition of consulting (from Chapter 4: "Being a consultant is nothing more than utilizing your skills and creativity, as well as having an unburdened nature to generate and capitalize on progressive opportunities"), you are unbounded and should certainly explore this source of contribution to clients and revenue to the firm.

Software and other tools can be a significant component of your business and can actually transform the business. Go with what works for you.

Creating solutions for the market utilizing software and other things of significance may require you to form a partnership with the vendor(s). That vendor has facilitated your development, and you may need to buy a run-time version of the software for the market, become a special kind of partner, and so on. If you're developing like this, you will likely want to be that partner because it will afford you access to the code, vision, and developers of the software.

DEVELOPING SOFTWARE FOR A CLIENT

If any development occurs on a client site or on a client's dime, you must be mindful to have an agreement with the client that you can spin the development off into your business and other clients. Sometimes this takes the form of substantially reduced or free services. Of course, nothing proprietary to a client should be used in the "market" version. Some clients will want an agreement that the software development will not be used at their competitors as well, which would erode their potential market advantage from the software. The further you get into generic and technical software and away from industry- and client-specific software, the less restrictive these covenants will be.

Action Plan

✓ Check your normal style of communication. Do you exhibit a healthy combination of get it over with, get it perfect, and makest thou me no waves? Classify your close acquaintances. Are you able to deal well with people who come from all styles?

✓ If you are considering a partnership formation, go through the partnership checklist with your partners.

✓ Consider the partnerships and the style of partnerships that you want to cultivate with vendors.

Chapter 16

Getting the Word Out

- The Campaign
- The Telescript and Being Prepared for Conversation
- The Target List
- Newsletter
- Action Plan

This chapter may seem to go against the grain of the advisement to win business by generating inbound calls. We're going to talk about doing outbound activity. This should be done in conjunction with activities designed to draw in business through guerilla marketing, managing relationships, and incenting others to do the same for your concept. However, again, do what works. If you are behind the curve in branding or contacts, you may be able to jump forward in actual business through a well-done campaign.

A well-done campaign consists of three things:

- A succinct message delivering a worthwhile value proposition that promotes a service

- A channel of communication, generally e-mail or phone

- A target audience list suitable for the message and able to spend to fix the problem addressed in the message

The Campaign

Coming up with a bounded campaign criteria can be a challenge. Literally, the world is your oyster, and the possibilities are endless. I talked about developing services in Chapter 6, and hopefully you heeded the advice and you keep having relevant services for your market. However, in order to understand which service(s) to promote in a campaign, you will need to understand the relative strength of the service. You may want to refer to your notes when you developed the service to refresh your memory on:

- The market for the service

- The size of the market

- The competitive landscape

- The title or function of the target buyer

- The value proposition for the offer

- Any collateral you have for the offer

When it comes to the message itself, it's important to keep in mind that we're all bombarded by messages these days. I spoke earlier of occasionally not answering my phone due to the volume of telemarketing coming through that channel. Likewise, I—like you, I'm sure—have spam filtering on my e-mail. Still, some spam gets through. Well beyond spam are the countless e-mails that don't really pertain to me personally or call me to action.

Some of it is opt-in marketing that I'll get to in less busy moments. Regardless, if you want to get my attention through e-mail or the phone, your message had better be targeted and convince me you might be able to help me solve a problem. It needs to do this very quickly, especially if I pick it up during a very busy time. It's surprising how frequently we tend to forget these rules and expect that the receiver of *our* messages has lots of time and was just waiting for our communication.

Consider the following sample e-mail text as one that should get attention:

```
I would like to introduce myself and my firm as a way to
maximize COMPANY NAME's investment in CRM technologies.
Bean Consulting Group is an experienced Microsoft Certified
Advantage Partner that helps enterprises solve the problem
of managing ever-growing information.

Redundant and conflicting CRM technologies expose organi-
zational inefficiency leading to wasted time and higher
costs. Managing the technologies is beyond a technical chal-
lenge, it's an organizational one. Business processes,
rules, and data quality must be addressed.

Bean understands these challenges. Our experienced consul-
tants provide frameworks around the people, processes, and
technologies necessary for CRM success.

CRM is one of our core competencies, as we have a signifi-
cant portfolio of deployment.

Please contact me with a time to show you how these projects
are more than paying for themselves in a challenging econ-
omy and what we can do to ensure you get your customer data
under control.
```

Actually calling on a campaign is 99 percent sheer boredom and 1 percent pure adrenaline. You need to be prepared for conversation, but you will spend most of your time talking to voicemails, finding out people have moved, talking to administrative assistants[1], and finding out people's roles are not what you thought, despite their title. Not everyone is cut out for executing this type of campaign or will decide it is the best use of their time, which is why outside telemarketing firms exist. (See the upcoming "Using Outside Telemarketing" sidebar.)

---

[1]Nothing wrong with this; you can get a lot of information from these conversations.

USING OUTSIDE TELEMARKETING

There are countless telemarketing firms that will call on your behalf. They will call as a sales representative from your company: John Smith with Hammer Consulting. Their objective is to get you meetings, and typically you will pay by the meeting, frequently with an upfront "retainer" that is applied to the meetings generated.

They "guarantee" meetings, which means you need to contractually ensure that if they do not produce the meetings, you will get your retainer back—or at least most of it.

The key is the ability of the telemarketing firm to relate to your business and convey it to prospects. For some businesses, this is almost hopeless. For some telemarketing firms, regardless of your business, this is hopeless.

I have yet to meet a telemarketing firm that did not claim they would understand my business and generate appointments. But few really did! They like to brag about successful campaigns done in a "similar" (in their view) industry. However, when put to the test, they seldom could convey my value proposition with 25 percent of the vigor that I could. I am looking for something on the order of 50 percent of my vigor—just around the opening sentences—and the ability to generate meetings.

If or when you find a telemarketing firm that can relate to your business, deliver the goods, and not upset prospects with an extreme short-term focus, that is like finding pure gold. You definitely don't want to shop them based on price alone—unless your business is *very* simple.

You will also want to provide them your complete telescript *and test them*. Don't let the gauntlet go down on the campaign until you approve the delivery. That's *your* reputation you are entrusting them with out there!

An example structure of such a program could be:

- This program is for delivery over 30 days, designed to generate 20 sales appointments.
- The consultancy provides a list of target market, potential customers, and names of any businesses that it does not wish contacted; Telemarketing 101 will provide the database for the campaign.
- Campaign is "pay for performance," with a campaign payment of $7,100 due upon signing and applied to the production of 20 sales appointments.
- Rate is $355 per appointment for the delivered 20 appointments.

> **NOTE**
>
> As a rule of thumb, on a calling campaign, you must have 25 prospect conversations in an eight-hour day. Talking to voice-mail does not count, nor does talking to the wrong person to hear your message, talking to administrative assistants who don't add value, and so on. Try to get *value* from *every* conversation you have. Value can come in the form of the name of a better contact or information about the company pertaining to your offerings, such as technologies deployed or being considered, budgets, growth cycles or areas, and so on.

Some campaigns are actually a combination of e-mails and calls. The conclusion in sample e-mail text earlier in this section does not commit you to call back, but it asks the recipient to call you. Of course, most won't. If you get three percent return calls or e-mails (and not the ones that say "Take me off your list!"), you are doing well.

A more aggressive approach is to conclude your e-mail with a specific time you will call. For example:

```
I will give you call on Friday, July 31, at 10:00AM so we
can talk in person about <company> and your CRM challenges.
```

I personally don't favor this approach because it commits me to call at that time. How much time do I allow for the call? Do I schedule them all 15 minutes apart? Is that enough time if I actually get the person on the phone? If I actually make it into a good conversation, do I ignore the call(s) that follow? Or do I try to set them 30 minutes apart, knowing that:

- Ninety percent will not be at the phone then for whatever reason.
- Of the 10 percent who do answer:
  - Fifty percent will not remember my e-mail.
  - Twenty-five percent will remember it but did not read far enough in the e-mail to note the time.

This leaves 2.5 percent of the conversations I am seeking. If I send 32 such e-mails with specific times, I could set them all in the course of one business day (assuming one set for every 15 minutes) and may get one good conversation. That's okay if you and your message are great, but you'd better have some other things to do that day that don't mind constant interruption. If a campaign targets well more than 32 (like most will), that's multiple days in this mode. That's tough.

A telemarketing firm can execute these types of campaigns because it's what they do, and their limited knowledge will not allow them to talk for more than 10 minutes anyway. Their job is to set up appointments for you. However, I find it awkward to set a time to call—as if it's important—and then the caller just tries to set up another call.

The Telescript and Being Prepared for Conversation

If you are calling, you need to be able to grab the person's attention quickly and keep that attention until you know there could be business or there definitely is *not* business with that person. Business, in this context, does not necessarily mean immediate business, but it could be future business with that person or someone he or she might know. In other words, if you are calling professional environments, be professional, be a good listener, and don't write people off until they tell you to. Most people will not waste your time, because that would also mean wasting their time.

Despite the fact that you know your business and your industry inside and out, you should build a telescript (telephone script), which is the message you will use to initiate conversation. For example:

> Hello. I'm John Russell with Security Services International. I'm calling you from Philadelphia. We are experts at security and compliance—that is, information protection, Sarbanes-Oxley, Six Sigma, and the like—and I was trying to reach whoever may be related to these types of initiatives at <company name>.

Don't "read" the telescript. It needs to sound (and be) natural. If you get a positive response, you should be able to take the conversation from there. You should be able to discuss your offerings and go into your value propositions. Again, I am suggesting that this is going to be the distinct minority of the calls that you make.

Also on the telescript, and accompanying you on these calls, should be a bevy of information that you can refer to should you need it. It's easy to forget all your value proposition points when they are not in writing. This includes:

- Brief and extended descriptions of key services
- A succinct biography of yourself, your key people, and the profile of people you tend to utilize
- Articles, webcasts, and podcasts that are available on the Internet
- Upcoming speaking engagements
- Familiarity with technologies, methods, processes, and so on that may be interesting to the prospect
- Guiding principles
- Customer lists
- Differentiators
- Competitor list and your competitive points for each one[2]
- Questions to ask *them* to learn more about their situation and engage conversation
- A list of likely objections and your response for each

SPEAKING OF OBJECTIONS

Speaking of objections, there are a number of standard objections that you are likely to hear. Although your specific comebacks to these will depend heavily on your consulting value proposition, in general the aforementioned ROI approach (from Chapter 1) tends to cut through most of them as best as possible.

If you are truly offering the customer minimal investment with measurable short-term ROI, why wouldn't they do it? The reasons fall into these four categories:

- They don't believe the service has the ROI (in which case, you should work on the service).
- They can't make any investment. (Make sure you have tight ROI cycles in your service.)
- They don't believe you can deliver the ROI with the service. (It's hard to tell where the difficulty may lie here.)

Be prepared to state the links you want to share. If they are long or difficult to state, make tiny links at www.tinyurl.com.

---

[2]Don't disparage the competition. It's in bad taste. They have a place, too. Be prepared to describe what situations they fit best in and what situations you fit best in.

■ You are misfiring with a value proposition they don't relate to.

Of these objections, not having budget (Objection 2) is the most difficult one to overcome, but keep focus on the return, on the short-term and long-lasting nature of the return, and on how it will help the person meet his or her objectives.

Identifying the common objections to your message, refining your service as a result, and tightening up your message are important parts of a campaign.

The Target List

Who you target on your campaign is vital as well. Even more so than the message and the medium, the target list is very specific to your area of consulting focus. Think not only about who you would love to talk to (or have read your e-mail) about your campaign, but who you are likely to get to *listen* or *read* your information. Often, we'd love to talk to the CEO about our value proposition, but chances are you are not going to get the CEO's attention. They often have a serious filtering system in place because they are bombarded. You may have to target a level that you may actually have communication with.

For many companies, you will have a hard time finding people's names below the senior executive level, so your messaging may contain a strong element of, "Would you please pass this along to whoever is in charge of the _____ program?" This may be necessary, but expect a drop off in response, since it involves the message taking an extra hop.

Telemarketing firms can pull lists according to your criteria. However, if you're not using a telemarketing firm, where are you going to get your list? You can buy lists, as I have done, but expect the data quality of that list to be around 60 percent. That is, around 60 percent will be good names, associated with the company they are at, with a current title and phone number. The rest is just the old stuff you'll have to slog through. Like the telemarketing firm you find that works for you, finding a good list for you is also like finding pure gold.

List-pulling can be like teeth-pulling if you do it record by record, as in through Internet search. There are services available where you can do research for a fee. These list service brokers include Hoovers, Dun & Bradstreet, and OneSource. These services keep up the information they broker. The data quality is more like 95 percent. As a member, you can enter the parameters and pull your targeted list into Microsoft Excel, ACT!, or whatever tool you're using to store the information for the campaign.

The parameters you have at your disposal include:

- Industry and sub-industry
- Company size (by number of employees and annual revenue)
- Public/private
- Title
- Geography

For example, you can target all senior marketing executives at public healthcare companies in the Midwest region.

INTERNATIONAL EXPANSION

You may want to consider a geography outside your country, especially if you do research and determine that another country is significantly (that is, three-plus years) behind in terms of its consultants' capabilities to deliver the services you do, *and the need is not that significantly (that is, one to two years)* behind. Of course, the travel issues (in other words, costs) are exacerbated. However, an "expert from afar" air about you could help your candidacy. This "expert from afar" aura, though clichéd, is going to be well deserved in your case.

Many utilize international assignments or even an international move to accomplish some lifestyle goals of spending time abroad.

NOTE

There are techniques for maneuvering within organizations by phone to get to the right person. If the receptionist will not help you, you can dial randomly within the company's phone number ranges. When you eventually get a live person, you can probe for the names you really want. This is not worthwhile for a consultant to do for a cold call. However, if you believe you have a great proposition for their specific situation, you might try this occasionally.

In case you're wondering about e-mail marketing efforts to *your* known contacts, that is really more like a newsletter where you can be more colloquial in your language, because they already know you and (at least some of) your value propositions.

There are plenty of books on e-mail marketing, and I suggest you avail yourself of more information if you are serious about this method of marketing. However, if the approach recommended is untargeted, consists of primarily a discussion of getting "working" e-mails, and encourages provocative messaging designed to hook the reader, regardless of your particular value proposition, you are entering the world of spam (excuse me, "viral marketing"), and that has no place in a professional consulting practice. What these books may offer regardless is information on managing campaigns, creating interesting messages aligned with your value proposition, and using follow-up protocols.

OF COURSE I'M GOING TO CALL YOU

Once I was speaking at a conference, and I had a side conversation with someone. We spoke for 5 to 10 minutes, and I was giving him specific advice on his issues in relation to my topic and expertise. I had a line forming, so we did not fully finish the conversation. After the show, I listed him in my follow-up stack, and a few days later I called him. Most of the time, these calls are well received because there is more to the conversation and I am willing to give more advice. My upside is the hope that something exists at the client for which I could provide some consulting.

In this case, the person was downright hostile. How dare I call him? In his mind, the conference experience was totally divorced from his daily work, and he wanted full control over his interruptions. The call did not lead to business. But I did get up to bat and pursued the lead, as I always will.

We live in a business ecosystem where hibernation is not an option. If someone attends conferences, registers for webinars, gives out business cards, or is otherwise out there in the marketplace, he should expect to be called by the vendors with whom he interacts. Contact information is part of a value exchange for something that the person (hopefully) received. Most people understand this. You are going to get the door slammed in your face a few times, but if you are generally not upsetting people, you should pursue targeted business.

> **NOTE**
> Don't be Machiavellian[3] about campaigns. Even if you get some business, if your message is insulting or offputting to 95 percent of those who read it, overall you have failed in your firm's objectives.

Newsletter

In a newsletter sent to people you have met, you can use more colloquial language than the formal language used in a marketing campaign to cold prospects. Of course, stay professional.

Timing is important in consulting, so you never know when your newsletter may intersect a customer's need for your services and the newsletter becomes the spark that leads to business.

Some elements of a successful newsletter include:

- Industry overview
- Industry news
- Company overview and general update
- New services or service update
- Recent collateral, articles, presentations, blog entries, and so on that are now available
- Call to action

In every newsletter, give the reader the option to opt out of your newsletters—and, at their request, take them off the list for the next ones.

Even though the reader knows you and will be more apt than a cold prospect to actually read the information, because of our aforementioned busy schedules, the information should be kept brief. Include a brief call to action, such as, "Call today to learn more." Say (and mean) that you will be generally available to take people's calls and e-mails.

Action Plan

✓ Determine whether you will sign up for a list broker service.

✓ Develop your first campaign (message, list, medium) and its complete telescript and/or e-mail text.

---

[3]"The ends justify the means"—that guy.

Chapter 17

Marketable Value and Exit Strategies

For those of you who start your own firm, eventually, there comes a time when your status as grand poobah of Joe's Consulting will come to an end one way or another. It could come to a sudden end due to health reasons, family reasons, IRS reasons, a divorce, or other reasons beyond your control and foresight. Or it could happen due to a change in ownership. Or you may decide to sell all or part of the practice. In any case, you should plan for end game scenarios.

Consider the following end game scenarios for your status with the business:[1]

- Unexpected circumstances, such as IRS liens, divorce claims, or health-related issues
- A change in the ownership structure of the partnership
- Selling all or part of the business

That's Not a Marketable Business

Of course, here, it is important to distinguish that we are talking about something with actual value. If you have a guru-style firm (refer to Chapter 1), which has not scaled much beyond yourself, there is no equity involved. This does not mean you are not supremely valuable to a new job situation; it's just that your compensation will most likely be found in your base and bonus calculations and perhaps a sign-on bonus, as opposed to anything more complicated than that.

I once had an employee candidate say to me that he needed an upfront lump sum of $400,000—this was in addition to a healthy salary after that. His rationale: He had two years of making $200,000 on his own as a consultant, and the going consulting firm valuations were two times annual income. Let me expound on the absurdity of that statement to make a point.

Some of this may seem obvious, but when it comes to one's career, sometimes emotions take over, and it becomes hard to have empathy for the other person in a discussion. The other person—in this case, me—is asking, "What's in it for my firm and

---

[1]Practice leaders at larger firms typically get revenue sharing and equity as spelled out in an employment agreement, which also usually states that if you need to leave the company, the equity all stays with the firm.

my clients?" So, while it's nice that Joe has made $200,000 on his own for two years, given his salary needs, even continuing that (on his own, within the firm structure) would prove a year-over-year wash inside a firm. Where's the excess income? Outside of Joe, there is no revenue stream. Without mincing words, from my perspective, that's not a marketable business.

I can get five percent (let's say—for round numbers) on my money in the bank. That's $20,000 a year. Plus, I would get my principal money back anytime I like. Investing in Joe is much riskier, not to mention the sheer competitive situation for the position. By the way, hopefully you can do better than five percent on your money by investing it within the business (in other words, in salespeople and selective consultants before they get into the black, marketing, infrastructure, and so on).

EMOTIONAL ATTACHMENTS TO THE BUSINESS

One time I went to one of those stores that makes large quantities of shirts with logos on them. I wanted to get my company logo on some shirts to give away to employees, clients, family, and so on. I went to an inexpensive place that actually turned around some sample shirts quite quickly. When I returned to see the samples and looked at the shirt, I nearly cried.

The workmanship was awful. The logo was unrecognizable, and the two words were unreadable. It wasn't even sewn down onto the shirt very well. To see the representation of my "baby" treated with such disrespect was emotional for me. I was surprised at my reaction. And it was just a shirt!

Emotional attachments to the firm do happen and are a large reason why people do not consider their alternatives.

Business Valuation

When it comes to business valuation, eventually something has to make money in the market. Or at least that is the idea. Unlike the bank account example, a small business purchase is like purchasing an indeterminate cash flow. To truly value the purchase, the buyer would have to make his or her best stab at the cash flow and put a value on that. However, many will take shortcuts in the process and use simple valuation measures.

> **NOTE**
> Consider the Ponzi scheme crafted and executed by Bernard Madoff. Investors weren't able to track their "investments" to the point where somebody was making some money from an activity. Consider the implosion of the banking system in 2008/2009. Simple, middle-income American mortgages were leveraged to the hilt. One quote I saw said that every dollar was leveraged 30 times! So, here we had 30 entities expecting to benefit from a mortgage payment. It's no wonder the market generated more and more mortgages. Anyway, we saw where that got us—to a house of cards. I expect a heightened sense of real value—for a while.

Of course, both sides should be hoping that synergy between the parties will lead to even better things for the entity. In other words, the combination of forces should not mean 1+1=2. They should mean 1+1=3. The buyer will want to base the price on what you have done to date—and this is probably the fairest position. However, the selling firm will want it based on what they will do within the new concept. When I talk about the structure of the purchase offer, we'll see how this often gets addressed—with an "earn-out."

If you wish to leave your business for a job and your firm is below threshold, you can sell your accounts payable and the hard assets and head back to corporate life.

Many consultants ask me what they should do in order to sell their business. For most of them—mostly below the $1,000,000 mark in revenue—the simple answer is to grow the revenue and get concerned with it when you get closer to the threshold. As a rule of thumb, the gray area between a "that's not a business" and a business with marketable value is at about $5,000,000 revenue. Less than that, usually you will fall into the camp where you may get a sign-on bonus and you may get an agreement to continue to receive a high percentage of the gross profit of outstanding accounts receivable. However, buying companies are less likely to want to invest in the paperwork and due diligence around a company purchase for a smaller company.[2]

That minimum watermark may go as low as $2,500,000 in a great economy where there are synergies—and where you insist

---

[2]Sometimes the buying company is the smaller company, but usually not.

it be a company sale as opposed to a sign-on bonus situation. In a very poor economy, the minimum revenue a purchasing company may consider could be as much as $10,000,000. In a very poor economy, companies are usually simply not in the market for other companies. If they are, the valuation is impacted.

> Making a certain amount of revenue can allow you to entertain the idea of selling—having conversations and further discussion with prospective buyers.

The valuation is based on quite a few variables, which market conditions clearly have an immense impact on. Sheer revenue is not nearly the only measure. Gross revenue is also very important, especially when the valuation lacks much non-cash strategic value and the purchase is about cash flow.

I will give you some more rules of thumb here, but a very important thing to keep in mind is that there is more art to it than science. Anytime anybody says anything about this subject, somebody can raise their hand and say, "Yes, but I know about ABC company who did it this other way." That variability in valuation and even revenue and other minimums that secure interest is indeed borne of art, negotiation, timing, the economy, moods, the price of tea in China, and untold numbers of variables.

True business valuation is what a willing buyer will pay for something. It's nothing more than that. There are no laws on the books to help either side with a valuation. There is no consumer protection for you should you wish to be a seller or a buyer.

Consider the conditions under which you may be eligible, what selling and various other exit strategies you may want to have, and what the process is like.

Timing Is Everything

Even if monetary considerations are primary for you, selling the business may not be the right way to go. Valuations tend to expand as revenue and other measures go up, so you may find your firm on the higher end of the valuation metrics after you grow a while. You also may find yourself in a worse economy, where companies have less to spend and are scrutinizing purchases more. Or the opposite may be true. And your business could have an upturn or a downturn.

> My recommendation is not to wait long after you have achieved threshold and have marketable value, recalling that pigs get fat and hogs get slaughtered.

Considering two important variables only—your revenue and the economy—see how valuations can change.

Year	Revenue	Economy	Valuation
1	$1M	Good	0
2	$3M	Good	0
3	$5M	Good	$7M[3]
3	$5M	Good	$10M
4	$7.5M	Good	$15M
5	$10M	Good	$20M
6	$10M	Good	$22M[4]
7	$10M	Fair	$17.5M
8	$7.5M	Fair	$10M[5]
9	$5M	Fair	$6M
10	$5M	Poor	$4M
11	$7.5M	Poor	$6M
12	$10M	Fair	$15M[6]

Over time, last year's revenues become less interesting, and an overall revenue average may be more interesting, giving some added weight to recent years. Of course, if the firm makes it to 10 years, 20 years, and so on, it's almost a proven concept, and buyers are less likely to discount the valuation due to fear of a downturn. This is true as long as the firm has been innovating and is not stuck in a technology or an approach that is fading. Even those firms will have some value, but as prospects for the thing you are known for diminish, hope of future growth diminishes as well in the eyes of a buyer.

Stay relevant and innovate for maximum value. What's hot today may not always be.

Hopefully it goes without saying, but the values in the table are strictly hypothetical and only consider two variables. Again, true valuation is what a willing buyer will pay.

Timing is important. The market may be ready, but, as you can see, there are many reasons why you may not be.

---

[3] Lower valuation due to lack of track record at the $5M level.
[4] Now that the firm is above the mental threshold of $10M for two years, a kicker is added to the valuation.
[5] You're trending down and so is the economy, so your valuation is getting dinged.
[6] You may be back to the Year 5 mark, but you've proved it can go lower.

From a nonmonetary perspective, which is quite important when considering this topic, your prospects may include companies that you and your team, knowingly or unknowingly, may not be a fit for.[7] How might a buyer not be a fit? Oh, let me count the ways:

1. Culture

2. An overbearing boss (kind of like the one you left behind in corporate life)

3. Bureaucracy

4. Location

5. Contractor approach versus consultant approach (refer to Chapter 1)

6. Incompatible vendor relationships

7. Client profiles by size

8. Client profiles by industry

9. Selling approach of services first versus products first

10. Custom versus one-size-fits-all mentality

In other words, it's all the factors that always determine whether someone is a fit at a company. However, in a company sale, you are likely going to be required to stay at the company for a certain number of years, so fit becomes more important.

Valuation Metrics

You may have noticed that a "good economy" valuation being used in the examples (once a track record is established) is two times revenue. That's fair, although many will get more if other factors are in place. Sellers like to cite five times revenue as the metric, and it's true that was the case in the overheated economies of the mid-1990s, when it looked like everything was going to work despite the odds and everything was going up forever. However, the scuttlebutt is now more back to two times revenue, but that could clearly change with time—up *or* down.

In some cases, the other factors that need to be in place have to do with direct synergy, and other times they have to do with indirect synergy. Sometimes it's good to represent something that the firm does *not* have in any shape or form. That can make for a

---

[7]As mentioned later, in consulting sales, you and your team usually work at the new firm for a number of years.

smoother transition because your concept will not need to merge at the practice level with the firm's existing practice.

It's better to have a practice that is synergistic with the buying firm at some level. For example, you both do Java programming. However, your firm does it better, and you've gotten further faster as a result. Better in this context refers to market positioning, contacts, length and size of average client relationships, vendor relationships (in this case, with Oracle Corporation), and so on.

So, synergy is one other important factor, which may be considered a "soft" factor. Other soft factors are those from the prior section relating to good personal fit for you and your team. You're not the only one who will be checking out these factors. The buying firm also will, and they will value appropriately.

Back to the math: Revenue is not revenue. A buyer cannot take your revenue to the store. You take the after-expenses part—the owner's salary, dividends, and retained earnings. If this "gross profit"[8] to the business is less than 30 percent, prepare to get dinged. If it is greater than 30 percent, congratulations—you will receive higher consideration.

Profitable revenue talks. Unprofitable revenue walks.

An ROI valuation, not unlike the one cited in Chapter 1 when I spoke of using ROI with client situations, is another method a buyer might use. What will your firm, treated as an "annuity," pay the buying firm, and how much is one of those annuities?

These are some metrics. I'll spare you commenting again about it being an art and true valuation borne of true offers. (Oops—I didn't spare you, did I?) You may wonder how to get past the metrics and get one of those market numbers.

Remembering all those sales you made over the years? Well, here's one that may take more of your time and be the most complex sale you've ever made! In actuality, the factor similar to your business sales (hopefully) is that you are not looking for a churn-and-burn sale, but a real fit. This fit is very important and very personal. It will take time. Your firm's business must allow you that time—and not suffer because of it!

You might use a business broker to facilitate the effort (see the "Business Brokers" sidebar), or you may make some inquiries on

---

[8]Also known as EBITDA—earnings before income taxes, depreciation, and amortization.

your own and find some traction. You might get some incoming phone calls about your business from brokers or (hopefully) prospective buyers. This is a good indication that you may have something to sell. You should take those calls, listen, and learn.[9]

BUSINESS BROKERS

I have sold two businesses without a business broker and one with a business broker. The idea is not much different from selling real estate. Fees are usually 10 percent of the selling price. Although there is no way I could personally think of, contact, and find all potential buyers of a consulting business, the universe of potential buyers is still quite limited, and with some research and effort on your part, you should be able to find some prospects on your own. Consider (relatively) larger firms with business synergy that have purchased other companies recently. This way, you are not the guinea-pig company they attempt to purchase, only to find out all the peculiarities and details associated with buying a company and eventually bail out of the process.

To Sell or Not

All this talk about selling the business—as if it's everyone's goal. It's not, nor should it be. You may wish to establish a practice you can run at your pace (low, moderate, *or* high) until Mother Nature stops the process. This serves the function of keeping you productively busy and hopefully having fun and challenge, which are extremely important to life, in addition to income.

You may also wish to have a firm that you bring your children into. In an unsure future economy that can turn very quickly, passing along the most efficient path to success in consulting and your chosen field of application is perhaps one of the best things you can do for your children.

You may have developed practice lines in your firm that have marketable value and less interest for you. You could sell off those lines and keep your core business. However, all the criteria in this

---

[9]What goes around comes around. Do not play people. If you're interested, talk. If not, politely say so. You still may learn some things and establish a contact for the future.

chapter (minimums, valuations, and so on) apply to just that line—the part you wish to sell—and not to the entire firm.

Business sellers tend to reap some financial rewards and satisfaction because they created something of value out of nothing, but only you (and your partners if it's a partnership) can decide what is right for you. You may also take into account the opinions of your key employees (and so might the buyer).

One good reason to sell is to quickly gain access to more resources that you can utilize to increase your client's abilities to improve their business. Another good reason is to help your employees get more stability, without losing the cultural aspects they enjoy.

The Deal

You should be happy with the cash at closing as full price. All future events, such as the company stock rising, are unpredictable.

Cash at closing is king. Everything else needs to be discounted in its value. This includes future cash (although that's usually pretty solid), bonuses, and definitely stock.

Your cash in the business usually remains with you. Outstanding accounts receivable will be paid to you at closing or upon receipt from the clients over time. Current business, not yet in receivable status, usually goes to the new firm. None of this should be considered part of the price being paid for the firm.

The price paid for the firm is almost a misnomer because it has multifaceted components.

The tax implications of all of this are serious, and you should have everything reviewed by your accountant. In particular, you want the tax treatment of the sale price to be considered capital gains and taxed at the lower rate (assuming it's still lower when you read this).

Once high-level terms have been agreed upon in principle, you can expect to be taken under a letter of intent, which outlines the agreed-upon terms but also gives the buyer—and your team—a certain number of more days, usually 60 or 90, to perform more due diligence. The letter of intent is an offer "subject to completion of due diligence satisfactory to both parties," so therefore it is not a document indicating finality to the deal. I once was under a letter of intent, but the deal did not materialize. The letter is designed to give both parties the comfort that both are serious and can open the books entirely to the other entity.

Usually the firm is bought. However, sometimes it's the assets only, and you end up keeping what's left of the firm after the assets are bought.

At this point, if not before, as part of due diligence, the buying firm may request to speak with your key employees, key clients, and possibly key vendors to ensure that they will not be running to the hills if the transaction completes. They want to be sure that none of these will be disturbed by the new relationship. You should exercise control over the process, knowing that once anyone is brought into the process, they know of the intent to sell. This could comfort them vis-à-vis the new resources at their disposal. However, it will most likely be a surprise, even if you've alluded to it, and may cause some discomfort at first. This is a human reaction that needs to be dealt with, with all the earnestness you can muster.

The buying firm may want to lock down key employees into employment agreements themselves. If your employees and the firm cannot come to an agreement, the deal could be jeopardized. The buying firm will also want to review all contracts (with employees, contractors, and clients) to understand which terms carry over and which ones do not. They need to know what they're buying.

You will also be promising not to make any major changes to your business between the letter of intent and closing without the firm's consent. In effect, the firm is now your board of directors. At some point during the letter of intent period, if due diligence is satisfactory to both parties, the transaction completes, and you, your team, and so on are now part of Bigger Firm, Inc.

> The purchase agreement is complex, perhaps hundreds of pages. I've only touched on the high points here.

You will most likely have a one-, two-, or three-year employment agreement, in addition to the agreement to purchase the firm. This agreement specifies how long you must stay with the new firm. Hopefully, you have selected each other well enough so that this isn't important, but realistically I know of several employment arrangements that expire with the employment agreement. The length of agreement the buyer wants is usually related to the degree you are personally involved in running and/or representing the business. As a rule of thumb, the larger the business, the less you are going to be seen as personally needed.

> If you don't want a long employment agreement, actually act on that old maxim in your practice now—be working yourself out of a job.

The employment agreement is not unlike any other employment agreement. It specifies your salary, title, role description, variable compensation, benefits, any grounds either party may have to terminate,[10] noncompetes, nonsolicits, and confidentiality

---

[10]The employer may have a "for cause" clause, which, if triggered, can have a bearing on amounts already paid to you for the business.

agreements. If you do not have a lawyer review this, you are being foolish.

THE ATTORNEY IN THE DEAL

Well before you get this far, you should have engaged an attorney for advisement on the negotiations (which occur well before you receive a *bona fide* offer). You should engage a good sell-side attorney for small business. (It does not have to be consulting.)

Make sure your attorney does not seem like he or she is going to (1) kill the deal unnecessarily or (2) drag it out unnecessarily. Some attorneys are just inclined toward these objectives. Remember, it's your life. Attorneys provide a tremendous service to you in terms of how purchase contract language is going to be interpreted by the courts. A buyer will surely have an attorney. However, just as in a real estate transaction, that attorney is not your attorney. Your attorney is the one you pay.

The process for accountant selection in Chapter 4 is all relevant here in attorney selection as well. Don't be afraid to shop around and change if necessary.

Most likely, you have had to work with an attorney in the practice leading up to this point. That attorney may or may not be the best attorney for working with you through this phase. Check his or her qualifications.

Hopefully, you have followed my advice and kept great records along the way. You're going to need them for selling all or part of the business and for taking on or removing partners.

The sale of a company can be excruciating, with lots of false starts, seemingly unending petty requests, and the baring of your very soul to strangers. In the end, if it has allowed you to better serve clients, then it is worth it.

Action Plan

Now, in the first 90 days, think about your exit strategy.

Chapter 18

Parting Words

- It's Not What You Make
- Save Some for Me!
- Riding the Roller Coaster
- Buying Self-Determination
- Giving Back
- Less Than All-In Consulting
- Ethical Issues
- Have I Held Back?
- Final Thoughts
- Action Plan

Regardless of where you are in your consulting journey, I wish you the best. The first 90 days are crucial. Hang in there. You are potentially growing, and hopefully you believe there is nothing wrong with that. We can healthily appreciate how our former employers have shielded us from all the challenges of the "real world" while accepting the challenge, opportunity, and rewards that consulting can provide.

It's Not What You Make

It would be unconscionable for me to exclude the topic of your relationship with money in a book that's at least partly about making money. I simply don't believe you are going to enjoy your experience in consulting without developing a healthy relationship with the "filthy lucre."

I have focused on making income with consulting. Without the income, we have no further conversation. If you follow the direction in this book, 95 percent of you will be earning more than you ever have. You will easily be in the top five percent of income earners in the world. When you reach the $500,000 gross income level, you are assuredly in the top one percent of income earners.

Then again, when it comes to income, perhaps you have realized some of your marketable value through realizing an exit strategy.

In my role of advising you about what is best for your consulting business, I have recommended healthy yet prudent reinvestment in the business (refer to Chapter 14). I have done the same regarding your time, getting you to recognize your time split between various activities (refer to Chapter 1).

Yet, there is still that discretionary income and discretionary time, and it would seem that is what we are doing so much of the rest for. Again, I will mention that you should find consulting fun such that it does not seem like a pure "investment" of your time. The intangible rewards are plenty. However, I acknowledge that we care about making money and believe that a healthy relationship with money is essential when working for yourself—either in your firm or your practice in a larger firm—in a profession with very high income potential.

It surely will not do your business any good for you to struggle in your personal finances. Some new consultants, believe it or not—

and this could be you—will struggle with the esteem factor around making more money than they ever have before. If you were making $50,000 in your pre-consulting job, and now your consulting presents you with the opportunity to make $250,000 or $500,000, you simply may not see yourself as worthy and may subconsciously make the moves necessary to keep you in your comfort zone, which is perhaps $75,000. This is more than what you were making, yet not nearly the potential of your concept.

These issues can go deep, well beyond my expertise. I do acknowledge it and have seen it a lot. If you find yourself hitting some walls in your consulting, perhaps the problem is mental. Are you following all the advisement from this book? If not, why not? Are you making prudent growth moves? Are you concerned about not being "one of the boys" from your pre-consulting days? Do you think you'll feel more pressure on yourself to keep it up once you get there?

Sooner or later, to maximize your potential, your frame of reference around money needs to be readjusted from non-consulting to consulting. Hey, do you need me to tell you how much some of the richest people in the world make?![1] They make more than I ever will and probably more than you ever will. I'm not founding a software company that is going to control operating systems and hit the market at just the right time. I'm not an investment wizard or an heir to a fortune.

Now do you feel okay about making your measly top-one-percent income of $500,000? Good. Don't read the next sentence if you're still squeamish.... Consulting is one of the top earning professions in the world, with its top practitioners making on par with surgeons, top attorneys, chief executive officers of public companies, and riff-raff like that. Okay?

I've acknowledged here that you are most assuredly not going to become the richest person in the world doing this. I don't really know how to advise you to become that, nor do most of the people actually doing that advisement. My $500,000 gross income target for you, through to the $1,000,000 mark, based on sound and proven principles, is about where I stop. Once you clear that hurdle—and want to go further—let's compare notes.

Put consulting in context. It's not going to pay like you're an oil tycoon, but it's pretty darn good...if *you* are.

---

[1] See the *Forbes* annual Forbes 400.

Save Some for Me!

So I'm acknowledging that I am leaving some for my fellow humans. Try telling me that 15 years ago! Take it from me now: Somebody's going to kick your butt out there (in other words, beat you in a deal, get a better offer from the same client, and so on) in the short term. The best approach is to try to outlast those suckers like the tortoise outlasted the hare.

Even at that, somebody is going to kick your butt in the long run. This may occur through better application of these principles, through better positioning or having a better foundation, through better timing or a better market, through deciding to live in a better geography for his/her concept, or through sheer dumb luck! Don't kill yourself over this fact. There is always someone better _____ (fill in the blank) than you or I at something, but would it be trite to say that only you can be the best you? At the end of the day, that is going to have to rule the day.

I'm going to do my best to provide more client value than my competition. My experienced consulting colleagues are also not going to step aside for new entrants. They are going to use their experience, their wits, their skills, their political abilities, their broader contexts, and their contacts to win engagements against you, just as they do against me.

Come on in. The water's warm. But watch out for the sharks.

Consulting does come easier the longer you do it. However, there are ups and downs on its roller coaster.

Riding the Roller Coaster

The roller coaster refers to the financial and mental ups and downs you experience over the course of time in consulting. Every day, week, month, quarter, and year are different. Some quarters, your energy will go into billing at one client site, trying to fix a broken situation, running a large project, or perhaps just hoping to spark some more business from the client. Other quarters, you will have several clients you are doing yourself, or perhaps you have teams on the ground that you can barely triage without doing any personal billing. And then there are the lean quarters when you not only are low in client count and prospects, but you have some employees on the bench, with you (and them) getting nervous about their pay.

Income and gross income will fluctuate in consulting, which was cited in Chapter 17 as a valuation issue. All things being equal, you would like some consistency to your finances. From a strict valuation perspective, it does not look good to have a booming quarter followed by something that is 10 percent of that quarter. Of course, you appreciate the boom! But you have to question your concept when you have a large drop off.

> Income will fluctuate, but if it's by 50 percent or more quarter over quarter, you really have to question your concept.

Rather than delve back into these challenges specifically, which is what the rest of the book is about, I'll say the solution to all consulting problems is to do consulting right. You may not get this until you gain some experience. It's kind of like addressing health problems by being healthy, which includes the whole routine—healthy eating, exercise, sleep, vitamins, stress management, and so on.[2] Experienced consultants will tell you that they run an overall good business, and that's what gets them through.

Speaking of the financial roller coaster, more of you are going to have my next money problem than will have the prior one. This is the problem of personal spending. You make. You spend.[3] You make more. You spend more. You make less. You…are stuck.

Your income will fluctuate as a consultant, much more than that of an employee. Your personal spending should be tracked to a reasonable measure of income—not necessarily the peak and certainly not where it is going, but where it is. You set your spending state of mind when you are at more modest levels. Hopefully, this means a commensurate modest level of spending and a habit that you can carry forward to your high consulting income. That's not always the case.

Some people overspend whether they have a little or a lot. Others will overspend once they get a lot. We all know the stories of lottery winners who return to their pre-winning net worth in short order due to overspending, bad and wrong investment choices (greed), and quite possibly doing it all by listening to the wrong voices—suits getting their piece of the action and/or their pre-winning and poor family and friends who are ill suited to give advisement.

---

[2] I'm not doctor, mind you—this is just a theory/example.
[3] I'm distinguishing spending from investing here; investing also refers to paying for necessary labor when your time is more valuable than being spent doing that labor.

It's your money, and you can do with it what you wish. You may find you have the opportunity to become a conspicuous consumer with consulting. You know—the big house, the fancy cars, the Rolex, the country club membership, the select sports for the kids, the luxury vacations, the fine wine, the private schools, and all that. I'm not knocking it! I do some of that. Again, it's up to you. Some of you have medical bills, elder care, or other real necessities that have to be taken care of. However, I suggest that one of the first things you want your money to buy is what I'll call self-determination.

> Consulting is a journey, just like life. You need to enjoy it.

Buying Self-Determination

Self-determination is not sold in stores. There is no money-back guarantee, blue-light specials, or "but wait, there's more!" It's about having control of your life to do with as you wish. It's about relieving your mind of the mental stress of financial worries and allowing it to remain creative about fun, family, and capitalizing on and creating new opportunities. It's about not taking big risks if you don't want to. And this all has to do with the lost art of saving and conservatively investing your money.

It has to do with finding what it is that truly makes you happy. Money doesn't buy that, but it can (what you keep, not what you make) buy self-determination by knowing you and your family will be taken care of and you can weather the ups and downs. I do put things such as being able to do less than all-in consulting if and when you wish, college for the kids (if you choose to pay for it), and so on into the boat of taking care of family, by the way. I'll stop on this subject—or save it for another book—but please make sure your discretionary spending is *truly* toward things that are helping make you happy, not toward keeping up with the Joneses.[4]

> Consulting is a lifestyle. It's work and play together. Eliminate strict divisions in your life.

Sure, consulting is fun—and I can never see not doing it!—but there are a lot of other things in life that aren't exactly consulting. Use your creativity to work them into a consulting lifestyle.

---

[4]If there's fun and happiness in that, I've yet to find it; I see it as more frustrating than anything else.

> ### THE GRAND DISAPPOINTMENT
> I'm taking some extra steps in the advisement around consulting, especially as we close the book, to make sure you use it to guide yourself toward happiness. The money that is made in any profession is not going to cut it. I'm elaborating on something that may help make you happy (consulting, not money), but happiness could evade you if you expect it to appear magically through any means. Happiness is a separate objective well worth pursuing.

Giving Back

I'm a capitalist at heart. I believe that the companies I help make more profits for create jobs for people who are willing to work, who in turn provide for their families, and that is a good—no, great!—thing. They also provide products and services that improve the human condition; sometimes those are conveniences, and sometimes they net new life options for people.

I believe some of my spending is helping those who make, prepare, ship, market, and sell the products, as well as their families—and that is also a great thing. You can, too, and you should be proud of that. I just find that some charities are even closer to the real thing when it comes to helping. There are also causes that can get neglected in our world that I find important and that need some direct help outside of the system.

On the subject of discretionary income, may I impose where I have no right? This is more personal than related necessarily to consulting. I'm also stretching a bit from helping you handle the money you make in consulting, but I feel it's important to take this opportunity, human to human, to remind of the hurt in the world, felt by more than we usually care to believe or acknowledge. I can't solve it all, but I like to do my part. I'm not kidding myself—it's part of that happiness quotient I spoke about earlier. But maybe it's part of yours, too.

It's not what you make, it's what you keep, give back, and truly enjoy.

I consult for the usual things, but the charities I choose to be involved in are part of that. If you feel the same way, don't forget the less fortunate.

Less Than All-In Consulting

Consulting is one of those things where, when the time is right, you can put the brakes on and keep some semblance of it going. Many retirees have skills, but consulting those skills has not hit their radar. If that fits you, congratulations on investigating this opportunity. If you're happy, that's what it's all about, so I'm not knocking anyone's happiness. However, if someone is not happy, maybe that person is lazy or lacks a consulting framework.

Is it reasonable for most 60-year-olds to start their consulting career? Yes and no. I say yes because I see no reason why not...but I also say no because of the mental hangups accumulated over years working in a more controlled environment.

> Consulting can work at providing different levels of rewards for different needs.

Less than all-in consulting can take place at any time. It's not just restricted to older folks. You may hit your number and find that, despite your creativity and tweaking, you can't make it as fun as some other things in your life.

Ethical Issues

From time to time, you will be faced with a situation where there may be an expedient result if you compromise the truth. In consulting, you will likely exercise a far greater number of transactions than you ever did as an employee, thus putting you in quandaries that you may need to think about *before* you actually experience them. Consider the following situations, which I suggest are ethical in nature.

- The client overpays (yes, it does happen), and you keep it all.
- In the heat of doing the transaction, you forgot to mention you'll need to charge for travel. The contract was signed without any mention of it. You bill expenses.
- You have the opportunity to utilize travel expenses that you didn't actually accrue and send them to the client.
- You're billing by the hour, but you spent some hours doing work for other clients.
- You're billing by the hour at a decent rate, but some hours just aren't very productive, due to lethargy. Or, you are starting to mimic the trends you see around you from the employees and blend in.

- You're doing a multi-city trip, but your clients believe you are doing the trip just for them. You have the opportunity to double-expense the travel expenses.[5]

- You go under an NDA and receive some prereleased information. You're seeing another company or vendor and want to look smart, so you drop some hints from your learnings that are going to make you look good when the events play out.

- You take your family on a business trip. They have to eat too, so you put their expenses on your expense report.

- You take your family (or you meet friends or family on a business trip) and go overboard in terms of what you would usually spend on a meal—because of your personal business.

- Your firm is not the only firm at the client. Your client expects your frankness in reviewing the other firm's work. However, they have promised you some other work either overtly or otherwise in exchange for a good report to the client.

- You are assessing a client situation and receive all you need from one or a few employees at the client. Your report looks like a regurgitation of their ideas, but without attribution.

- You repurpose another client's deliverables for a client, yet bill for time you would have spent if you didn't have the other client's deliverables.

All these situations and more ethical situations could hit you in the first 90 days, but they (or permutations of them) will undoubtedly find their way onto your path in consulting if you do it long enough. I have encountered all of these and more. In each case, the situation is written in exactly the *wrong* way to handle the situation.

Even if it means some extra trouble with the client's accounts payable department, you should never expense anything that was not spot-on to the client. If you are not providing top-tier consulting to a client (and for that client) for any hour, do not bill for that hour. Respect your NDAs—written and implied—and always give your frank advice to the client. And finally, if you reuse thoughts and deliverables, you don't get to bill for their initial work effort. Your rate should reflect your portfolio of talents, experiences, and your efficiency.

You must cover your income and cash-flow goals with ethical business practices.

---

[5]Many ethical issues in consulting revolve around travel expenses!

You may get away with some of these indiscretions in the short term, but you have started a slippery slope. Either you really are completely ethical or you are not. Good ethics are not just considered right by many, they are good business practices. They are on par with doing great work for a client. You do the great work, and it pays off in the short and long run. It's called repeat business.

Have I Held Back?

Have I spilled all my consulting beans, or have I held a few back from you? I've held some back.

Thinking about what I've held back from the book, it is mostly ideas I have that I haven't tried yet, that are too risky to share, and/or that I think just happened to work for me or others, but I really can't explain why other than dumb luck. It would not be a wise use of the real estate here to talk about things that most likely will not work. Does that mean I don't try them? Not at all—and you shouldn't necessarily refrain from trying them, either. What I have laid out here are the solid, foundational principles of effective consulting, backed by experience.

I have some marketing and delivery ideas now that I look forward to trying out in the real world. They are derivatives of the direction given here—everything is, really—but if I had to lay odds, I would say that they most likely aren't going to work. However, you don't know until you try.

They are boom or bust ideas. I don't think a consultancy can survive on a solid diet of boom or bust ideas, especially ones that go bust. I've recommended establishing your consulting in the first 90 days with proven principles. However, if you need to fork off of any idea herein, especially to accommodate unique characteristics of your industry, by all means do so.

Consulting is art and science. By design, it's mostly the science that is taught.

The critical skill is judgment. No one can teach that. We can only teach the skills, ideas, and tradeoffs you need to consider. Just as I mentioned before that every day is different, so is every decision. Every decision is made with the backdrop of a different set of inputs. Your sound judgment, keeping an eye on your goals, will need to rule the day.

Perhaps you will land on something unique that works very well. Give it a ride as long as it is working for you. And don't spill the beans. If it works, others will find out and copy you. Let them work at it. You still may be the best at it, and your judgment is necessary to determine when to shift direction.

> Do what works. Repeat until it doesn't.

The other reason some goodies are held back is that in my practice of consulting to consultants, I will be providing them in a value exchange, not unlike this book. I hope to provide more to you. Do keep in touch with me at www.90daysconsulting.com.

Final Thoughts

Before I close, I have a couple of parting thoughts. I hope it came through, but just in case it didn't, I want to impress you with the enormous value of people to your practice. On the employee/contractor side, I am continually amazed at the disincentives that consultants put to work in retaining good work. Many naturally do the corporate thing and put in place penalties for failure but no reward for risk. These folks are your lifeblood and can be a catalyst in your (and their!) growth and success. Take care of your team.

Likewise, your clients are to be treated with the utmost respect and care and are entitled to your very best hard work, service, and candor. The engagement process is one thing; the delivery is another. Whatever the financials used to engage a client, if you agree to them, you owe a high standard of service to that client.

In a consulting career, you will do well to encounter a few thousand clients (people). Some will do equally well with far fewer. It's not the numbers that count. Whatever the circumstances—and they're always unique—that bring together you with a client, you won't be able to go back in time to recollect the lost time should the relationship take a hit. In other words, don't have a "grass is always greener" mentality. Those are your clients. They are your clients for a reason. Take care of them.

There are so many varying preconceptions about consulting. Some will come into it with the idea that once they start their practice or have some small wins, the world will acquiesce, and they can then exercise a large ego in the process. Nothing could be further from the truth. Humility is essential. Put your ego aside and keep an objective eye on yourself and your practice. Take care of yourself.

Action Plan

✓ List your life priorities.

✓ List 10 reasons why you would like to be a consultant.

✓ Get your personal finances in order.

✓ Revisit the consultant profile you chose in Chapter 1 for confirmation/change.

✓ Bookmark www.90daysconsulting.com.

✓ Consider the ethical situations presented and others you believe you will encounter in your practice.

✓ Run a good consulting business.

Index